D1068414

9 COMMENTARIES ON FRANK LLOYD WRIGHT

9 Commentaries on
FRANK LLOYD WRIGHT

Edgar Kaufmann, jr.

THE ARCHITECTURAL HISTORY FOUNDATION
New York, New York

THE MIT PRESS
Cambridge, Massachusetts, and London, England

© 1989 by the Architectural History Foundation and The Massachusetts Institute of Technology
Printed and bound in the United States of America.

Library of Congress Cataloging-in-Publication Data

Kaufmann, Edgar, 1910–1989
    9 commentaries on Frank Lloyd Wright/Edgar Kaufmann, jr.
        p.   cm.
    Includes bibliographical references.
    ISBN 0-262-11144-6
      1. Wright, Frank Lloyd, 1867–1959—Criticism and interpretation.
    2. Architecture, Modern—19th century—United States.
    3. Architecture, Modern—20th century—United States.
    I. Architectural History Foundation (New York, N.Y.) II. Title.
    III. Title: Nine commentaries on Frank Lloyd Wright.
    NA737.W7K28 1989
    720′.92—dc20
                                         89-17495
                                             CIP

Edgar Kaufmann, jr., was Professor Emeritus of History of Architecture at Columbia University.

Alfred Willis originally compiled the bibliography on the occasion of the Temple Hoyne Buell Center's symposium on Fallingwater. It has been expanded for the present volume. The Architectural History Foundation is grateful to Gwendolyn Wright, director of the Buell Center, for permission to publish the bibliography.

Marco Polo describes a bridge, stone by stone.

"But which is the stone that supports the bridge?" Kublai Khan asks.

"The bridge is not supported by one stone or another," Marco answers, "but by the line of the arch that they form."

Kublai Khan remains silent, reflecting. Then he adds, "Why do you speak of the stones? It is only the arch that matters to me!"

Polo answers: "Without stones there is no arch."

Italo Calvino, Invisible Cities

Contents

Edgar Kaufmann, jr., died on July 31, 1989, just a few weeks before this book went to press. The present volume is thus not only a final record of his ideas and knowledge, but also a tribute to his memory.

Introduction

Brief, in-depth studies are, I believe, the best way to approach the works, the life, the ideas of Frank Lloyd Wright, at least until a more exact understanding is achieved. A scholar today comes to the riches of Wright materials with alien habits of mind and eye, even of soul (or psychology if you prefer). Then, all too easily the living power of Wright's art, of his faith in it, can disappear. For more than a quarter-century I have tried to present microanalyses of elements of Wrightiana, and here they are assembled, old ones and new. Professor David De Long helped me to improve them.

I am particularly grateful for the unflagging help of the staff of the Architectural History Foundation and to the Department of Architecture and Design at the Museum of Modern Art, New York. The Avery Memorial Library, Columbia University; the Burnham Library of the Art Institute, Chicago; the Buffalo and Erie County Historical Society; the Chicago Historical Society; and the Western Pennsylvania Conservancy all provided valuable material. In every case this was due to the goodwill of individuals who know my thankfulness. The *Journal of the Society of Architectural Historians* permitted the reuse of six essays. The oldest have been revised in wording but not in thought; I acknowledge their initial crudity. Perhaps over the years a sharper view has been achieved, but more important to me is the hope that I have come closer to Wright, to his architectural development. The Frank Lloyd Wright Memorial Foundation as always provided assistance vital to any understanding of the American genius.

'*Form* Became *Feeling*,' A New View of Froebel and Wright

Writing with great freshness for his book *An Autobiography* (published in 1932), Frank Lloyd Wright told how Froebel kindergarten training awakened his delight in the play of color and design. Then Grant Manson published well-regarded studies of Froebel influence on Wright's mature work. Richard MacCormac reexamined the matter ten years later, while Stuart Wilson wrote about the Froebel system per se. Other commentators have relied on these three, why reopen the topic? First, discrepancies among the various statements remained unresolved. Next, little has been known of the antecedents to Wright's childhood experience; he naturally trusted impressions gleaned from his mother, who died in 1923. Now, recently assembled information allows a clearer understanding of Froebel's role in the development of Wright's architecture.

To begin with two questions: was the first kindergarten in the United States opened in Boston in 1860 by a veteran of the American Transcendental movement, Elizabeth Peabody, or in Wisconsin under Germanic auspices in 1855 or 1856? Different authorities give different answers. In those early years was there a link to Wright's Wisconsin family, the Lloyd Joneses?

Valid information came from a small book published in 1908, Nina C. Vandewalker's *The Kindergarten in American Education*, alas printed on poor paper. The one copy available was on the verge of disappearing, hence two brief chapters, II and III, are reprinted here, documenting the introduction of Froebel's ideas into the United States. Around the fateful years 1848–1849 two young sisters, Bertha and Margaretha Meyer of Hamburg, studied with Froebel; then they went on to open the first kindergarten in England in 1851. The next year Margaretha married a fellow exile, Carl Schurz, and with him emigrated to America where Schurz rapidly made his way as journalist, politician, and patriot, associated with Abraham Lincoln. The Schurzes, joining others of the family, lived some fifty miles west of Milwaukee in Watertown, Wisconsin, where Margaretha gave regular kindergarten instruction to her own and neighbors' children, beginning mid-1856.

Eight or ten miles back toward Milwaukee lay

Reprinted from the *Journal of the Society of Architectural Historians,* May 1981.

the village of Ixonia where the Lloyd Jones family from Cardiganshire had settled in 1845, when Wisconsin was still a Territory. In March 1857 they moved farther west again to the Spring Green area. I have discovered no trace of contact between the two families. They may easily have remained unaware of each other; each was part of a cohesive immigrant group cherishing its native language, faith, and habits. Moreover, the Welsh Joneses were farmers first and collaterally teachers and preachers, while the German Schurzes were bourgeois idealists. All the same, the Joneses were actively progressive like the Schurzes, and both families had faith in self-reliance and in education. The Joneses had staked all on the Unitarian creed and adhered to it firmly in the New World. If they had word of Margaretha Schurz's work, only a few miles away, Froebel's underlying theme of a unitary universe exemplary of God could make a strong appeal. And if so, young Anna, eldest of the three daughters in the family who were to become teachers, would not escape hearing of the kindergarten doctrine.

As the years passed she surely heard about it since German settlers throughout the Middle West promoted Froebel's ideas and adapted them to the needs of their communities. These ideas were debated at regional meetings of professional educational associations, and in such circles Anna Lloyd Jones met her future husband, William Russell Cary Wright. It becomes difficult to believe that Anna Wright, by 1876 married and living in Weymouth, Massachusetts, went to the Philadelphia Centennial ignorant of the kindergarten movement. Preparations for the kindergarten demonstration at the fair, begun a full year before under Ruth Burritt of Wisconsin, were reported in Elizabeth Peabody's *Kindergarten Messenger*. This or some echo of it could well have drawn Anna to the fair despite meager means, while William stayed home with the children. In an annex to the Woman's Pavilion Anna Wright could watch the Froebel instruction in action and find that she could acquire the skills and afford the tools to strengthen in her son and daughter awareness of 'the Divine Principle of Unity' that was the basis of the Froebel method.

The Froebel method, firmly based, used a set of well-thought-through techniques, yet it was ever changing. Friedrich Froebel himself often refined and adjusted his practices and writings; it would be unrealistic to fix a standard version of the method. Thus it is pertinent to learn what was available to Anna Wright as she trained in kindergarten instruction. Unfortunately, Stuart Wilson's investigations, which might have helped, were limited to Froebel texts of the 1890s, accenting the system differently than similar texts fifteen or twenty years older.

How did the Froebel method present itself to Americans in the mid-1870s? Mistrusting the traditional emphasis on book learning, it sought to foster harmonious growth throughout the child's whole being. Humans and the environment were considered parts of the same creation, the 'Divine Unity.' Thus young children might learn to feel competent in, and respectful of, the world opening up around them. These ideas were spread by Froebel's adherents; his own writings were not translated until after the Philadelphia fair. Froebel instruction in 1876 was disseminated by books and periodical articles, admirably traced in Chapter III of Miss Vandewalker's record. How much of this was available to Anna Wright is not known but she probably made use of Elizabeth Peabody's *Kindergarten Guide,* 1863, reissued 1864, 1870, and 1874, the authoritative book at that time. It included "The Moral Culture of Infancy" by Miss Peabody's sister, Mrs. Horace Mann, which may easily have appealed to Mrs. Wright.

In Miss Peabody's guide music, play, gymnastics, and dancing come first. Then follow the 'occupations,' play organized into games; these involve 'gifts,' that is, materials prepared in accord with the rules of the games. Repeated simple dimensions gave regularity to all the 'gifts': colored papers slotted for interweaving in strong patterns; cards pierced so yarns could be threaded through, again patterns in bright colors; slender sticks with peas as joints, for orderly constructions in space; paper for three-dimensional folding; and then the geometric forms — spheres, cubes, cylinders, and rectangular or, rarely, triangular blocks, ready for grouping in patterns. These groupings followed two rules: strict symmetry and no leftover pieces. Moreover, the assemblage could take place on a special tabletop ruled in squares, and then the pieces were expected to lie along these lines. Colored, flat cardboard shapes also included some diagonal edges but still were keyed to the grid. Later on the training continued into elementary geometry, elocution, the relationship between opposites, the relationship between senses and mind, and production of simple practical objects.

In the Froebel 'occupations' spatial play was limited to stick constructions and paperfolding. Covered enclosures could hardly be made with the blocks; they were not presented as building blocks, but as regular geometric solids said to underlie the complex shapes of nature and of familiar man-made objects: "shapes lay hidden behind the appearances all around" (*An Autobiography*). Frank Lloyd Wright, nine when his mother introduced the Froebel training, and his sister, seven, would have found more of interest in the relatively advanced work. Anna Wright, daughter and sister of Unitarian preachers, encouraged by her minister husband, would have emphasized the unity underlying God's creation.

What did Frank Lloyd Wright record of this episode? *An Autobiography* was written from the later 1920s on; he was evoking memories of half a century before. The main passage concerned with Froebel training divides into two segments. The first re-creates his mother's reaction to seeing the Froebel presentation at the fair; the second, longer one reports his memory of the experience at home when Mrs. Wright was guiding her children according to kindergarten methods. "Mother made a discovery"; chances are the discovery was how to apply the Froebel method, not the fact of its existence. Milton Bradley's, a company which distributed Froebel 'gifts' and manuals, is mentioned. No doubt represented in Boston, as said, its headquarters were in Springfield. Lastly, the Froebel display at the fair was located not in the 'Exposition Building' but in an annex to the Woman's Pavilion.

Wright's own memories follow an expectable sequence. Much about brightly colored papers, then the peas-and-sticks constructions, then the maple blocks and a significant phrase: "so *form* became *feeling.*" A mast is mentioned from which to rotate pendant 'spheres, cubes, and triangles' (demicubes). Then come the flat, slant-edged red cardboards. Lastly, Wright mentions the polished tabletop but not the ruled grid on it. Nothing about songs, play, or dances, or about the more advanced mathematical or philosophical concepts.

What of Wright's references elsewhere to the square grid marked on the top of the Froebel table? Throughout his writings he traced to it his use of modular planning, likening it to the warp and weft of weaving. An expanse of regular modules did nothing to impede free composition, but helped the proportioning and rhythm of his plans and, sometimes, elevations. It also led to a constancy of measure suited to the mechanical preparation of building parts, for example, wood trim, prominent in Wright's early work, or later his 'textile block system,' precast concrete shells strengthened by reinforcing rods introduced on site. The regular grid was a device, a tool of architecture which Wright used like his often-cited T square and triangle. It guided his design but did not govern it.

Others have noted that Wright's main passage about Froebel training follows immediately on a longer, more developed one recounting an early fascination with his father, alone, playing Bach and Beethoven late into the night. Often the young boy had to pump the airflow of the organ during these reveries. He learned from his father about the structure of music, and naturally he associated musical structure with emotions aroused by the composers. Here, perhaps first of all, form became feeling for Wright. This dual childhood experience with musical and with abstract visual compositions enforced Wright's consciousness of the pro-

found interdependence of design and expression. Furthermore, both music and the Froebel "occupations" relied on underlays of regular repetition, the beat and the module. "Usually you hear music as you work," Wright aged sixty wrote in "The Logic of the Plan."

The image presented here differs essentially from those of Manson and MacCormac. Manson deserves credit for his pioneer study of Wright but he was content to point out the similarity between illustrations in Froebel manuals and the exterior forms of Wright's works. He was trapped in a dogma of the day, form for form's sake. Thus he ignored statements by Wright and Froebel not concerned with form, and he had no clue to the power, or the limit, of Froebel's influence on Wright.

MacCormac realized the need to revise Manson's presentation. His essay in the *Architectural Review* is evenly divided between an assessment of Wright's development and specific analyses of eight Wright buildings from 1892 to 1908. MacCormac states that Wright began to design masses, influenced by Froebel illustrations, and that later he acquired a feeling for architectural space. That is not confirmed in the record. Wright's words, quoted by MacCormac, are: "This sense of interior space, made exterior as architecture, transcended all that had gone before." Wright was describing the growth of his architectural self-awareness. Buildings, drawings, and photographs that document this development make clear how gradual was Wright's long progress. From his earliest independent work in 1889 his architecture had been spatially engendered; what then required years of development was Wright's fluency in the expressive handling of space.

MacCormac claims that Froebel gave Wright a philosophy, a design discipline, and a characteristic style. One needs to forget Wright's family heritage, especially the strong Unitarian doctrine, if Froebel is to be the one responsible for rousing the nine-year-old boy's "powers of reason" and "sense of the harmony and order of God." Froebel's angular blocks — we have seen how they were but part of a system — were packaged as a compact cube, to be taken apart and the elements differently assembled by the child. MacCormac equates this with Wright's desire for an architecture which was "instead of many things, one thing," but that is the opposite, joining various elements together as one whole rather than taking a whole apart into many elements. The blocks, butted together, are said to have given Wright a sense of interior space; if so, miraculous!

MacCormac's analyses of individual buildings are based on the foregoing ideas, and each example is examined as if the plan, or superimposition of floor plans, reveals its essence. Only a few of MacCormac's strange judgements will be mentioned. The Blossom house of 1892, moonlighted while Wright was still in Sullivan's employ, is the first example. Its nearly symmetrical plan is related to the light, tight, neocolonial exterior, as MacCormac points out. However, the somber Arts and Crafts living hall is thoroughly asymmetrical. Awkwardly, the space of this interior elbows up a wide stair shaft whence light flows down through a screen of balusters. Directly opposite, an unsubtle large window competes for attention. The house and its plan are not understandable until this and

other immaturities are taken in account. The 1907 Tomek house is used to demonstrate a longitudinal plan Wright "had begun to adopt in preference to the symmetrical, cruciform plan" attributed to Froebelian precedent. But the Heller and Husser houses of a decade earlier, both illustrated, are far more longitudinal and asymmetrical than the Tomek. Throughout this half of his essay MacCormac features his 'tartan,' that is, syncopated, grid, said to be at the root of all these plans. Recently H. Allen Brooks, a preeminent interpreter of Wright's designs, pointed out that what MacCormac did was to eliminate some lines from the regular grid gratuitously. In fact, Wright used 'tartan' grids infrequently and then loosely. One can compare MacCormac's gridding of such early plans directly with Wright's own shown and explicated in his article, "The Logic of the Plan." The two minds are far apart.

What then can be said of Froebel's contribution to Wright's architecture? Wright's recollections should be considered in the context of his full architectural development. Froebel could not help in concepts or relationships of space, which were paramount to Wright. He added nothing to Wright's masterly ordering of platform, wall, and roof. But he could teach how compositions benefit by adapting to an even field of modules. He could endorse Wright's search for a universal value in architecture, for ways to unite humankind, shelter, and environment in harmony. And then, Froebel awakened Wright at the onset of his sensibility to the essential poetry of visual arts, "*form* became *feeling*." Wright's debt to Froebel is different and deeper than has ever been claimed by investigators up to now. "Here was something for invention to seize and use to create."

PRINCIPAL SOURCES

H. Allen Brooks, "Frank Lloyd Wright and the Destruction of the Box," *Journal of the Society of Architectural Historians,* March 1979. Comment cited occurs in caption to FIG. 14.

Chester Lloyd Jones, *Youngest Son,* Madison, Wis., 1938. Privately printed. Best record of the Lloyd Jones family, endorsed by Maginel Wright Barney, the architect's sister. Wright is not mentioned in this book.

Richard MacCormac, "The Anatomy of Wright's Aesthetic," *Architectural Review,* February 1968; and "Froebel's Kindergarten Gifts and the Early Work of Frank Lloyd Wright," *Environment and Planning B,* 1, 1974.

Mary Mann, *The Moral Culture of Infancy,* and Elizabeth Peabody, *Kindergarten Guide,* Boston, 1863, 1864; and New York, 1870, 1874. Both printed together; listings show now one, now the other as main reference.

Grant C. Manson, "Wright in the Nursery: the Influence of Froebel Education on the Work of Frank Lloyd Wright," *Architectural Review,* CXIII, June 1953; and *Frank Lloyd Wright to 1910, the First Golden Age,* New York, 1958. The book contains a more judicious version of the Froebel episode.

Elizabeth Peabody, *Kindergarten Messenger,* Cambridge, Mass., 1873 through 1875.

Carl Schurz, *Autobiography,* abridged by Wayne Andrews, New York, 1961. Contains scant information about Margaretha Schurz.

Nina C. Vandewalker, *The Kindergarten in American Education,* New York, 1908. The facts in this book hold up well, but I have used Carl Schurz's circumstantially detailed date for his settling in Watertown.

Stuart Wilson, "The Gifts of Friedrich Froebel," *Journal of the Society of Architectural Historians,* December 1967.

Frank Lloyd Wright, *An Autobiography,* London/New York/Toronto, 1932, 11.

Frank Lloyd Wright, "The Logic of the Plan," *In the Cause of Architecture,* New York, 1975, reprinted from *Architectural Record,* LXIII, January 1928.

Excerpt from Nina C. Vandewalker,
The Kindergarten in American Education,
New York, 1908.*

CHAPTER II
The Period of Introduction; Kindergarten Beginnings

The first kindergarten in the United States is popularly supposed to have been the one opened in Boston in 1860 by Miss Elizabeth Peabody, but the real beginning of the movement must be placed several years earlier and ascribed to a different source. The European Revolution of 1848, brought to the United States many Germans of culture and influence, who during the decade between 1850 and 1860 established private schools, bilingual in character, in all the larger cities in which their countrymen had settled,— New York City, Hoboken, Detroit, Milwaukee, Louisville, and several others. It was in these schools, based upon the principles of the new education, which at that time had found little or no recognition in the United States, that the kindergarten in the United States had its real origin. Although these schools did not attract from American educators the attention which their excellence deserved, and hardly a mention can be found of the kindergartens that most of them contained, their indirect influence in behalf of the new education in general and of the kindergarten in particular was considerable. The whole kindergarten movement in Wisconsin can be traced to the efforts made in its behalf by those in charge of the German-English Academy of Milwaukee, —an institution of the kind in question, and this is not an isolated instance. The German-English Academy at Louisville, Ky., and that at Detroit, Mich., as well as the institution in Newark, N.J. of which Dr. Adolph Douai was principal, did effective service in promoting the spread of the new institution. Although several of the earliest kindergartens were private and independent, the impulse that led to their organization came from the same general source. With the single exception of Miss Peabody's, the ten kindergartens established in the United States before 1870 all owed their origin to the movement in question. The first kindergarten in the United States was one in the home of Mrs. Carl Schurz, in Watertown, Wis., in 1855. The second was that opened by Miss Caroline Louise Frankenburg in Columbus, Ohio, in 1858. As far as can be learned, the first of the German-English institutions to adopt the kindergarten was Dr. Douai's school, to which reference has already been made. The kindergarten became a part of that institution in 1861. A kindergarten was opened in Hoboken, N.J., at about the same time, and three years later two were opened in New York City. One was opened in West Newton, Mass., in 1864 by Mrs. Louise Pollock. The inspiration of the kindergarten ideal came to

---

* Vandewalker's text is reprinted exactly from the original book.

Dr. William N. Hailman in 1860, during a visit to the schools of Zurich, Switzerland, and in 1865 he added a kindergarten to the German-English Academy of Louisville, Ky., of which he was president. It was in this kindergarten that Mrs. Eudora L. Hailman found the inspiration to her life work, and that she and her husband began their thirty years of united service to the kindergarten cause. The German-English Academy of Detroit adopted the kindergarten in 1869, and in 1873 organized effort in its behalf was undertaken by the German-English Academy of Milwaukee. There is little record of the effort made by these institutions or by the private kindergartens thus established to influence existing educational procedure, but the indications are that such influence was much more widespread than has been supposed.

The efforts made in behalf of the kindergarten by Dr. Henry Barnard and Miss Elizabeth Peabody, are fairly familiar to the educational public, but the relation between these efforts and those of the German exponents of the kindergarten has never been adequately shown. Dr. Barnard visited England in 1854 as a delegate to the International Exhibit of Education Systems and Materials, and while there became deeply interested in the kindergarten. English interest in the doctrines of Froebel had been awakened in 1854 by the lectures of the Baroness von Marenholz-Buelow, Froebel's foremost disciple, and by the practical work of Madam Bertha Ronge, who had been a pupil of Froebel and an active worker in the kindergarten cause in her native city of Hamburg. With Madam Ronge had been her sister, Miss Margaretha Meyer, also a pupil of Froebel. Dr. Barnard made a report of the educational exhibition in general and of the kindergarten in particular to the governor of Connecticut upon his return. He also described the exhibit of kindergarten materials in an article in the *American Journal of Education,* of which he was the editor. The report in question and the article, published in 1856, were, as far as known, the first articles concerning the kindergarten to appear in print in the United States. Between the time of Dr. Barnard's London visit and the publication of the articles, however, the kindergarten itself had appeared upon American soil. Miss Meyer had become the wife of Carl Schurz, and had come to the United States, settling in Watertown, Wis. In order to give her own children the advantages of kindergarten training she gathered together the children of relatives who lived near, and taught them the kindergarten songs, games, and occupations in true Froebelian fashion. This was, as has been stated, the first kindergarten in the United States.

Dr. Barnard's report concerning the kindergarten had awakened the interest of Miss Elizabeth Palmer Peabody, who is usually considered the apostle of the kindergarten movement in the United States. The interest thus awakened was deepened by an article which appeared in the *Christian Examiner* in 1859. This article, written by Mrs. Edna D. Cheney and Miss Anna Q.T. Parsons, was a description of the kindergartens of Germany and a summary of Froebel's principles as stated by the Baroness von Buelow. Miss Peabody at once undertook the study of Froebel, and a chance meeting with Mrs. Schurz during a visit of the latter to Boston in the winter of 1859 fanned her interest into a flame of enthusiasm. Having gained from Mrs. Schurz an insight into the practical details of conducting a kindergarten, she opened the kindergarten associated with her name the following year. "Miss Peabody had participated in the great social, literary, religious, and philosophical movement somewhat vaguely described as New England Transcendentalism," says Miss Blow, "and was peculiarly fitted both by natural endowment and experience to enter into the thought of Froebel." She was at this time fifty-five years of age, and in the full maturity of her powers. As sister-in-law of Horace Mann she had come into vital contact with the great educational movement identified with his name. She was a close friend of Bronson Alcott, in whose unique educational experiment she had shared. She had taught for years also in another private school of considerable note. That she gradually realized from the inadequacy of her results that the philosophy of Froebel needed a deeper study than she had given it; that she went to Europe in 1867 for the additional study which she considered necessary; and that she devoted the remaining years of her active life to the advancement of the kindergarten cause by teaching, writing, and lecturing, are facts well known to the student of educational history.

The significance for elementary education of the decade from 1870–1880 has already been commented upon. It was a significant decade for the kindergarten movement also, not alone because influences favorable to the kindergarten were set into operation at that time, but for other reasons as well. One of the indications of advance in the kindergarten movement was the establishment of kindergarten training schools, the first of which was opened in Boston in 1868 by Madame Matilde Kriege and her daughter. These ladies were pupils of the Baroness von Marenholz-Buelow, who had been induced to come to Boston by Miss Peabody. In 1872, Miss Henrietta B. Haines, the principal of a large private school in New York City, invited Miss Maria Boelte to open a kindergarten in her school. Miss Boelte was a pupil of Froebel's widow, who had achieved marked success both in England and in Germany. Her work in New York attracted much favorable attention. At the close of the year Miss Boelte married Professor John Kraus, already an exponent of the kindergarten, and together they established a kindergarten training school which is still in existence, although it has been carried on by Madame Kraus-Boelte alone since Professor Kraus's death in 1896. As trained kindergartners were thus becoming available, kindergartens multiplied rapidly. The kindergarten found a foothold in Washington, D.C., in 1870 through the efforts of Mrs. Susan Pollock, and its influence was strengthened in 1872 by the establishment of a training school under Miss Emma Marwedel. In 1873 several German kindergartens were established in Milwaukee, through the agency of the German-English

Academy of that city, and when the following year Professor W.N. Hailman succeeded to the presidency of that institution, kindergarten training was instituted also. The year 1873 saw the beginning of the kindergarten training movement in St. Louis, under the leadership of Miss Susan E. Blow, and the following year saw the beginnings of the movement in Chicago under the leadership of Mrs. Alice H. Putnam. In 1875 kindergartens were opened in Indianapolis and Los Angeles, Cal., and in 1876 in Denver and San Francisco, as a result of a lecturing tour by Dr. Felix Adler, who espoused the kindergarten cause almost from the beginning. The Philadelphia Exposition acquainted the Quaker City with the new institution, and when the Exposition closed, Miss Ruth Burritt, the "Centennial kindergartner," remained in Philadelphia to open a kindergarten and kindergarten training school. The kindergarten spread rapidly during the latter part of the decade, the result in part of the larger acquaintance with it for which the Philadelphia Exposition had furnished the opportunity. The friends of the kindergarten had recognized the opportunity which the Exposition would afford, and had planned accordingly. The Exposition kindergarten was conducted in an annex to the Woman's Pavilion, by Miss Ruth Burritt of Wisconsin, who had had several years of experience as a primary teacher before she became a kindergartner, and whose manner and insight were such as to gain adherents for the new cause. The enclosure for visitors was always crowded, many of the on-lookers being "hewers of wood and drawers of water, who were attracted by the sweet singing and were spellbound by the lovely spectacle." Thousands thronged to see the new educational departure, and many remained hours afterward to ask questions. The Exposition marked an epoch in the advancement of the kindergarten movement, as it marked an epoch in the history of elementary education.

The ready acceptance of the kindergarten after the Philadelphia Exposition did not imply a recognition of its pedagogical value alone; in fact it is worthy of note that many of the kindergartens established at this period were philanthropic in their ultimate purpose. As the rapid growth of cities and the increasing immigration was fast developing the slum with its attendant evils, people were beginning to realize that some antidote must be found. The value of the kindergarten as a child-saving agency was at once recognized, and churches and philanthropic societies took up the movement. The first charity kindergarten was opened in 1870 in the village of College Point, N.Y.; others were opened the same year in Cleveland, Ohio, and Florence, Mass. In speaking of this phase of kindergarten work in the Report of the Commissioner of Education, Miss Laura Fisher says: —

"Centering among, and concerning itself with, the children of the poor, and having for its aim the elevation of the home, it was natural that the kindergarten as a philanthropic movement should win great and early favor. The mere fact that the children of the slums were kept off the streets, and that they were made clean and happy by kind and motherly young women; that the child thus being cared for enabled the mother to go about her work in or outside the home — all this appealed to the heart of America, and America gave freely to make these kindergartens possible. Churches established kindergartens, individuals endowed kindergartens, and associations were organized for the spread and support of kindergartens in nearly every large city.''

The fact that kindergartens could be carried on successfully under public school conditions was satisfactorily demonstrated by the experiment made in St. Louis, Mo., by Superintendent William T. Harris and Miss Susan E. Blow. But for this experiment the general introduction of the kindergarten into the schools of the country — accomplished in large part during the following period — might have been postponed for many years. Dr. Harris was at this time acknowledged as the leading exponent of the idealistic philosophy in the United States, and as such he had actively espoused the kindergarten cause. Miss Blow was a native of St. Louis who had taken a course of kindergarten training in Miss Boelte's school. Superintendent Harris had recommended the adoption of the kindergarten as part of the school system to the St. Louis school board in 1870, but the first step in that direction was taken in 1873, when Miss Blow offered to superintend a kindergarten and instruct a teacher gratuitously, if the board would provide the teacher, the room, and suitable equipment. The offer was accepted, and the kindergarten was so successful that additional ones were soon called for. A training school was organized, as Miss Blow preferred to train her own co-workers, and new kindergartens were opened as fast as kindergartners could be trained. The success of the experiment made St. Louis the center of interest among school men, and educators from all parts of the country coming to visit, the stimulus was carried to their respective cities. Dr. Harris severed his connection with the St. Louis schools in 1880 and Miss Blow withdrew from the work that she had so successfully inaugurated in 1884, but by that time the practical value of the kindergarten as a part of the school system had been demonstrated to the satisfaction of the educational public.

The friends of the kindergarten movement in Wisconsin looked even farther than the introduction of the kindergarten into the public schools. They wished to secure its adoption by the normal school system of the state, and to provide for the training of kindergartners at state expense. Because of the many German residents of the state who had brought an acquaintance with the kindergarten from the land of their birth, the movement in Wisconsin had made considerable headway before it came into contact with the movement as it had developed in other sections of the country. In 1870 a vigorous campaign had been undertaken in Milwaukee which had resulted in 1873 in the organization of kindergartens in the four German-English institutions of that city. Professor William N. Hailman's acceptance of the presidency of one of these institutions in 1874 had not only strengthened the kindergarten sentiment among the German-speaking people, but had also brought it to the attention of the English-speaking people of the city and state. The first English kindergarten in Milwaukee was organized by Mrs. Hailman, and training classes were undertaken in both languages. A campaign for the introduction of the kindergarten into the schools of Milwaukee and into the normal school system of the state was undertaken. The second of these objects was accomplished during the decade under consideration, and the first soon after the opening of the following one. A kindergarten was opened in the State Normal School at Oshkosh in the spring of 1880,—"the first kindergarten officially and directly connected with any state normal school in the United States." A similar movement had been undertaken in Minnesota, and a few months later a kindergarten department was also opened in the State Normal School of Winona.

The organization of the National Educational Association in 1872 had afforded another means of stimulating interest in the kindergarten on the part of school men. At the first meeting Professor Hailman, then of Louisville, Ky., had presented a paper on: "The Adaptation of Froebel's System of Education to American Institutions," and urged the appointment of a committee to examine the system. The committee, consisting of Professor John Kraus, John Hancock, Dr. Adolph Douai, William T. Harris, George A. Baker, J.W. Dickinson, and William N. Hailman, made a most favorable report the following year, and the impression made by the report was strengthened by a paper read before the Association by Mrs. Kraus-Boelte. In the years immediately following, the cause of the kindergarten was kept before the Association by Mrs. Kraus-Boelte, Dr. Harris, and Professor Hailman.

At the end of the decade the friends of the kindergarten had abundant reasons to rejoice at the progress of the cause. In 1870 there were less than a dozen kindergartens in existence, all save one established by Germans and conducted in the German language; in 1880 there were not less than four hundred scattered over thirty states. In 1870 there was one kindergarten training school in the United States; in 1880 such schools had been established in the ten largest cities of the country and in many smaller ones. The year 1870 saw the establishment of the first charity kindergarten; in 1880 the new institution had become recognized as the most valuable of child-saving agencies, and mission kindergarten work had become so popular among wealthy young women as to be almost a fad. The practicability of the kindergarten as a part of the school system had been successfully demonstrated, and the logical sequence of its future relation to the school had been recognized by the establishment of kindergarten training departments in the normal school systems of two great states. The National Educational Association had set the seal of its approval upon the principles which the kindergarten embodied, and had commended the institution to the school men of the country for experiment and consideration. "The lessons of the Philadelphia Exposition, at which the meaning of the art and industrial elements in education was first revealed to the American teachers," had been taken to heart, and the result of the awakening it had occasioned had been the attempted enrichment of the elementary curriculum by the addition of the subjects frequently termed "fads,"—music, drawing, manual training, nature study, and physical culture. The fact that these subjects constituted an organic part of the kindergarten awakened interest in that institution on the part of many who had thus far given it but little attention. They began to see in the kindergarten games the true beginning for the child's physical development; in its gift and occupation exercises the foundation for art and manual training work; and in its garden work and nature excursions the foundation for a true knowledge of nature. The significance of the kindergarten as the logical foundation for a new system of education had therefore begun to dawn, and the comprehensiveness of the Froebelian philosophy stood out in striking contrast to the meagerness of the educational theory which then prevailed. The period of its apprenticeship was therefore over. Its advocates could silence doubt and criticism by pointing to results already achieved, and could urge its extension with the faith and enthusiasm born of the assurance that it met a recognized need in American life and education.

CHAPTER III
The Period of Introduction; Early Literature

The present familiarity with the spirit and method of the new education makes it difficult to comprehend the curiosity with which the first kindergartens were regarded and the difficulty that people experienced in understanding its philosophy. Even a slight acquaintance with the views generally held a generation ago will show that the difference between the views of life of the twentieth century and those of the period of the Civil War is worldwide. The idealistic philosophy, of which the kindergarten is the expression, considers the universe fundamentally spiritual, and nature and humanity as but varying expressions of the World-Spirit,— God. Man is therefore in essence good, and education is a natural process of unfolding his spiritual capacities, in accordance with the universal laws of evolution. This doctrine has permeated every phase of the world's thinking during the past quarter century, and no longer seems strange and unfamiliar; but at the time in question there had been little to familiarize the American people with such views. It is not surprising, therefore, that the kindergarten which embodied them should have appealed most strongly to the highly educated and spiritually minded in the early days and that its American sponsors should have been the New England Transcendentalists,— the American exponents of German idealism. The acceptance of the idealistic interpretations of the universe, reinforced later by the doctrine of evolution, then hardly yet formulated, and the new interpretation of Christianity in terms of social value,— these have given to the life and education of the present generation a depth and a significance that it lacked a generation ago.

The few, therefore, caught the real significance of the new institution in the early years;

the many saw, and comprehended but in part. Education in a guise so different from that which she had hitherto worn was practically unrecognizable. Visitors came,—too many for the well-being of the children or the comfort of the kindergartner; but, aflame with the enthusiasm of a new insight, she bade them welcome, hoping to gain new converts to her educational faith. The kindergartner of today, beginning work in a new locality, encounters few of these difficulties. She deepens the interest of the inquiring or silences the doubts of the skeptics by referring them to Froebel or his many interpreters, or by pointing to the results the kindergarten has accomplished in other localities. The kindergartner of the early day had no such resources. She must be, perforce, the priestess of the new cult, for available literature there was practically none. Froebel and his European exponents were hidden from the majority in the fastnesses of a foreign language. It is not surprising, therefore, that the translation of kindergarten literature should have been thought imperative and that the spread of that literature should have been considered an essential part of the movement. Had not the philosophy of Froebel contained fundamental truth it could never have kindled the enthusiasm needed to overcome the almost unsurmountable obstacles. The literature of the kindergarten, containing as it does the new philosophy of education in a nutshell, has been a significant factor in shaping educational ideals, and no study of the movement can be considered complete that does not include a resume of its development.

The beginnings were insignificant enough. The brief mention of the kindergarten in the *Journal of Education* in 1856 and 1858, and the admirable exposition that had appeared in the *Christian Examiner* in 1859, had, as has been stated, acquainted a few people with the existence of the new institution. Charles Dickens, the first great English student of the kindergarten, had written for *Household Words* in 1855 an article on "Infant Gardens," as kindergartens were called when first introduced into England. This article was written for the purpose of calling attention to the work of the Baroness von Marenholz-Buelow, who had come to England the year before to introduce the kindergarten system. "This article must always take a front rank as a strikingly clear, comprehensive, and sympathetic exposition of the principles and processes of the kindergarten," says Professor James L. Hughes. The Baroness herself had written a pamphlet on "Infant Gardens" also, and her co-workers, Madam Ronge and her husband, had written a "Practical Guide to the English Kindergartens." These articles had received considerable attention in the United States.

In 1862, an article in the *Atlantic Monthly* by Miss Peabody, entitled "What is a Kindergarten?" attracted further attention to the movement, and the interest awakened by the article and the kindergarten itself led Miss Peabody to the publication of her "Kindergarten Guide" the following year. This consisted of two parts,—an exposition of the kindergarten by Miss Peabody, and a treatise on "The Moral Culture of Infancy" by her sister, Mrs. Horace Mann, who had herself been a teacher and a co-laborer with her husband in his efforts for the advancement of education. About four thousand copies of the "Guide" were sold. The following year Mrs. Louise Pollock of West Newton, Mass., already mentioned, translated one of the German kindergarten manuals. She also wrote a series of articles concerning the kindergarten for a magazine called *The Friend of Progress*.

To familiarize the public still further with the kindergarten and with the educational principles that it represents, Miss Peabody wrote for the New York *Herald*, in 1867–1868, a series of articles upon the subject. The following year Miss Peabody, Mrs. Mann, the Baroness von Buelow, and others wrote a series of articles on the kindergarten and child culture in general for *The Herald of Health*. The editor of this magazine was Dr. M.L. Holbrook, "the first journalistic friend of the kindergarten." He had been connected with Dr. Dio Lewis in his efforts for the advancement of physical culture, and was at that time connected with the Hygienic Institution of New York City, which advocated the cure of the sick by hygiene and right living—a new idea at the time. These articles did much to acquaint a progressive class of people with methods of child rearing more rational then those which had thus far prevailed.

Among the leading contributors to the advancement of the kindergarten idea at this time was Professor John Kraus, a friend of Froebel, who had settled in San Antonio, Texas, in 1851. Professor Kraus had contributed to American journals frequent articles upon the Froebel-Pestalozzian methods, a series in *The Army and Navy Gazette* having attracted considerable attention. Recognizing the value of his acquaintance with the educational thought of Germany, Dr. Barnard had invited him in 1867 to become a member of the staff of the Bureau of Education. During the year he had contributed to the Washington papers a valuable series of articles upon the nature and purposes of the kindergarten. In 1870 and 1871 he translated a pamphlet by the Baroness von Buelow, and made an elaborate report upon the kindergarten for the Report of the Commissioner of Education. In this and other ways he helped to keep the kindergarten cause before the public.

To acquaint the public with the value of the new system of child training was one of the purposes of the friends of the movement during the early years, but another need speedily developed. As the demand for kindergartners increased and adequate opportunities for kindergarten training were still lacking, many with little or no preparation attempted to open kindergartens. It soon became evident that if these were to continue, technical instruction in the use of the kindergarten instrumentalists was needed. It was to meet this need that Mrs. Pollock had translated one of the German manuals in 1865, and that Edward Wiebe had prepared his "Paradise of Childhood" in 1869. It was because Professor Kraus and Mrs. Kraus-Boelte felt that these books did not sufficiently indicate the use of the materials and meet the needs of the many partially trained kindergartners that they undertook later what is undoubtedly their most important contribution to the movement, the "Kindergarten Guide," the first installment of which appeared in 1877.

During the decade between 1870 and 1880 several important books were written and translated. The first of these in order of time was "The Kindergarten; A Manual for the Introduction of Froebel's System of Primary Education into the Public Schools," by Dr. Adolph Douai of Newark, N.J., the principal of one of the first German-English institutions in the United States to adopt the kindergarten. In 1872, Madam Matilde Kriege made a free translation of the Baroness von Buelow's "The Child," and in 1873 Professor William N. Hailman wrote his "Kindergarten Culture." The lectures by which the Baroness von Buelow had converted Paris to the kindergarten cause were translated in 1876 under the title "Education by Labor," and her "Reminiscences of Froebel" was translated by Mrs. Mann the following year. Madame Kraus-Boelte's "Guide" also appeared during 1877. Several of Miss Peabody's lectures had appeared from time to time in pamphlet form. Through the translations of Miss Josephine Jarvis and Miss Fanny Dwight in 1879, Froebel's "Mother Play and Nursery Songs" was made accessible to English readers. The same year Dr. Holbrook translated and published "From the Cradle to School" by Bertha Meyer, and Mrs. Pollock a collection of "Kindergarten Songs and Games." All these helped to satisfy the increasing demand for a fuller knowledge of the kindergarten, and the philosophy of which it is the embodiment.

An important step in the advancement of the kindergarten was taken in 1873, when Miss Peabody established *The Kindergarten Messenger,* a monthly magazine of twenty-four octavo pages. This was especially needed at this time, as it acquainted the scattered workers with each other, and afforded a means of communication between them. In addition to reports from leading workers, correspondence, and general educational intelligence, it contained original articles, theoretical and practical, by leading kindergartners. The translation of "Reminiscences of Froebel," "Education by Labor," and other books appeared first in its pages. It gives a vivid picture of kindergarten conditions during this introductory period, and the personality of the gifted editor is felt in every page. It is a veritable mine of data for the future historian of the movement.

The fortunes of the little magazine were varied. In the Peabody number of *The Kindergarten Review,* Miss Emilie Poulsson says: "Miss Peabody had her struggle in maintaining the *Messenger.* The list of subscribers was never long, and not all of these were so good as to pay their dues. The editor records that one year it covered its own expenses, but that did not happen twice. Although all her own service was given free there was much financial worry connected with the enterprise, and she was often grateful for the kind help received from one or another of her friends." The *Messenger* continued through 1873, 1874, and 1875, but the next year it became a department of *The New England Journal of Education.* This arrangement, however, did not satisfy Miss Peabody, and in January, 1877, she again took the magazine into her own hands and ran it to the end of the year. As the thousand subscribers needed to meet expenses could not be obtained, it was merged in *The New*

Education conducted by Professor Hailman, then of Milwaukee.

The kindergarten interest that Professor Hailman had found existing in Milwaukee, and the financial support offered by Mr. Carl H. Doerflinger of that city, had enabled him to establish in 1876 the periodical in which *The Kindergarten Messenger* had now been merged. *The New Education* was an eight-page magazine, issued monthly. In the first number Professor Hailman thus stated the purpose of the new publication. "Froebel and Herbert Spencer are the principal exponents of the new education; the kindergarten, Froebel's great gift to man, is the first decisive practical step toward a realization of its requirements. To aid in the propagation of the views of Froebel and Spencer on education; to render the former, particularly, better known; to contribute in spreading the blessings of kindergarten culture in its genuine form and to make war upon all efforts for establishing spurious systems under cover of the honored name,—are the purposes of *The New Education*." Like *The Kindergarten Messenger* it contained practical articles for mothers and kindergartners, news concerning the spread of the new educational gospel, translations from standard German educators, discussions of current educational questions, and vigorous and incisive editorials. Its scope was broader than that of its predecessor, and it played a most important part in advancing the kindergarten cause and in shaping the educational policy of the Northwest during its formative period. Professor Hailman modestly ascribed much of the credit to the unwearying generosity of the publisher, Mr. Doerflinger, who for years sent the periodical free to the leading school men of the state. He says: "We have little doubt that to this generosity, aided by his personal effort as a member of the State Board of Normal Regents, Wisconsin is largely indebted for her present advanced position on the questions discussed in *The New Education*." After six years of existence it went the way of its predecessor, and was merged in *The Public School* of Boston. Like its predecessor it is invaluable for the educational historian.

The record of the kindergarten literature of the period would be incomplete without reference to the annual school reports of the superintendents in those cities which had adopted the kindergarten. Dr. Richard G. Boone considers that "the reports of school officers and educators include by far the largest part of America's contribution to the literature of education." He says: "But the most complete and systematic presentation of educational philosophy is to be found in the annual reports of Superintendent William T. Harris, while superintendent of the St. Louis Schools, from 1867 to 1880." Three of these dealt with the kindergarten. That of 1875–1876 discussed its philosophy; that of the following year the results of the kindergarten in the St. Louis schools, and that of 1878–1879 the history of the St. Louis kindergarten system. Although these reports seldom reached the general public, they were read by the leading school men of the country, and did much to shape educational opinion. The same is true of the articles on the kindergarten read before the National Education Association, and embodied in the reports of that organization.

No statement concerning kindergarten progress in the United States during this period would be complete without a reference to the two principal kindergarten supply and publishing companies, the Milton Bradley Company, of Springfield, Mass., and the Steiger Company, of New York City. Mr. Bradley's life experience had prepared him for conversion to the kindergarten cause in 1869, and through the improvement he has made in kindergarten material and the assistance rendered in the publication of kindergarten literature, he has won deserved recognition among kindergarten workers. Mr. Steiger, too, rendered valuable assistance during the early years. His confession of kindergarten faith was made in the publisher's preface to Madame Kriege's translation of "The Child." He says: "The Publisher of this book is resolved to expend his best energies in the interest of education. He has witnessed with lively satisfaction the progress of education in this country; but while appreciating the good that has been done, he agrees with the opinion of many that the system is capable of improvement. He has, therefore, embraced the cause of the kindergarten, as best calculated in his judgement to inaugurate a thorough educational reform; and he will gladly entertain proposals for the publication of other works on the subject and cheerfully cooperate with school authorities, associations, and individuals whose aim is the amelioration of existing modes of instruction."

If the friends of the kindergarten had reason to rejoice at the progress of the institution itself during the decade under consideration, they had no less reason for satisfaction at the increase in its literature. In 1870, there were in the English language, as far as known, but four books on the kindergarten,—Madame Ronge's "Practical Guide to the English Kindergarten," Miss Peabody's "Kindergarten Guide," Mrs. Pollock's translation of a German manual, and Wiebe's "Paradise of Childhood," a compilation from several such manuals. During the decade five important books had been translated in the United States,—The Baroness von Buelow's "The Child," "Education by Labor," and "Reminiscences of Froebel"; Froebel's "Mother Play and Nursery Songs," and Bertha Meyer's "From the Cradle to the School." Four books had been written,— Douai's "The Kindergarten," Hailman's "Kindergarten Culture," Madame Kraus-Boelte's "Guide," and Mrs. Pollock's "Kindergarten Songs." In addition to this, hundreds of articles had appeared in newspapers and magazines, and several pamphlets had been printed,—some for free distribution. The *Kindergarten Messenger* and *The New Education* had scattered the new ideas still farther. The seed-sowing was surely plentiful. The harvest will be traced in succeeding chapters.

Frank Lloyd Wright's Mementoes of Childhood

In a Note on Wright and Froebel recently published in this *Journal,* May 1981, I mentioned the importance of determining what Wright's mother could have known about Froebel practice in 1876 when she began to train her children by that method. It was therefore a delightful surprise when Bruce Brooks Pfeiffer, the archivist of the Frank Lloyd Wright Memorial Foundation, drew my attention to a small box in their files, adorned with Froebel images. It contained *An Illustrated Catalogue of Kindergarten Gifts and Occupational Material, together with a List of Kindergarten Literature, in German, English, and French,* issued by E. Steiger, 22 & 24 Frankfort Street, New York, in May 1876. FIGS. 1–14. Besides the catalogue, the box contained sheets of glazed colored paper, cut to allow interweaving in contrasting hues, and some examples of such interweaving. This was, in fact, "The Fourteenth Gift" listed in the catalogue for 20¢, including a dozen sheets in assorted colors. The interwoven patterns were in part neatly executed, and in part rather inept and tentative.

Speculation was hard to resist. Was this an

Reprinted from the *Journal of the Society of Architectural Historians,* October 1982.

example of the childhood play of Frank Lloyd Wright and his sister? Had their mother, Anna Wright, kept it, perhaps until at her death the architect took over her mementoes? There was nothing to guide such inquiries.

The catalogue, nevertheless, yielded positive evidence of the meaning attributed by Americans to the Froebel system in the mid-1870s. Most significant is a page devoted to the "Effect of the Kindergarten System," giving extracts from a report of the U.S. Bureau of Education. FIG. 1. This clearly confirms the secondary role of the geometric blocks in the entire Froebel method. Next in importance is the illustrated section entitled "Kindergarten Gifts and Occupation Material," dated May 1876. The twenty gifts shown illustrate "only part of my stock" as Steiger said, but they accurately present this aspect of the Froebel system then.

Throughout, there is no indication of architectural form or of spatial enclosure. From this one can deduce that Frank Lloyd Wright's recollection of Froebel training published in 1932 (the first edition of *An Autobiography*) was more authentic than those in his later publications, colored no doubt by outsiders' interpretations.

Furthermore, it is fascinating to read the list

Opinions of practical Kindergartners on the

Effect of the Kindergarten System,

from replies to inquiries by the U. S. Bureau of Education,

Washington.

(From the *Report of the Commissioner of Education* for the year 1874.)

"Physical development, manual skill, habits of clear thinking, order, precision, and attention." —

"Freedom and grace of movement, command of language, and superior preparation for public schools." —

"Development of the powers of application, perception, and reasoning." —

"Harmonious development; the mind is made active and the body is strengthened." —

"Excellent; minds clearer and quicker in acting." —

"Mental and physical development, and ability for self-occupation." —

"Beneficial to mind and body; all organs and powers are developed harmoniously." —

"It promotes a healthy and harmonious growth, a habit of attention, and a clear perception." —

"Mental and physical development and quickened observation." —

"Excellent progress without overtaxing the pupils." —

"Harmonious and natural development of every faculty, and strength, agility, and healthfulness of body and mind." —

"The best preparation for the common schools." —

"Habits of observation, correctness, and application." —

"Habits of attention, concentration, and obedience, and progress in studies." —

"The child becomes graceful, polite, self-dependent, skillful, thoughtful, constructive, and eager for knowledge." —

FIG. 1.   E. Steiger, *Kindergarten Gifts,* 1876. Effect of the Kindergarten System.

May, 1876.

Kindergarten Gifts

AND

Occupation Material.

NOTE. This Revised Price-List canceis previous Catalogues.

The First Gift.

For the youngest children:

Six soft Balls of various colors.

Aim: to teach color (primary—red, blue, yellow — and secondary or mixed — green, violet, orange) and direction (forward and backward, right and left, up and down); to train the eye; to exercise the hands, arms, and feet in various plays.

A Set, in Wooden Box, with Directions (*Frœbel's First Gift for Babies*), $1.00

Extra Sets, of 6 Balls, $0.60

Directions for the use of the First Gift may also be found in

HOFFMANN, *Kindergarten Toys and how to use them. A Practical Explanation of the first six Gifts of Frœbel's Kindergarten,* $0.20

and in many other publications.

The Second Gift.

Sphere, Cube, and Cylinder.

Aim: to teach form, to direct the attention of the child to similarity and dissimilarity between objects. This is done by pointing out, explaining, and counting the sides, corners and edges of the cube; by showing that the properties of the sphere, cylinder, and cube are different on account of their difference of shape; by pointing out that the *apparent* form of the sphere is unchanged, from wherever viewed, but that the apparent forms of the cube and cylinder differ according to the point from which they are viewed.

The forms are of wood, machine-made for this special purpose; are neat and provided with the necessary staples and holes for hanging.

In Wooden Box, with cross-beam for hanging the forms, $0.70

For **Directions** see HOFFMANN, *Kindergarten Toys,* and other publications.

E. Steiger, 22 & 24 Frankfort St., New York.

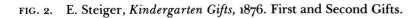

FIG. 2.   E. Steiger, *Kindergarten Gifts*, 1876. First and Second Gifts.

2　　𝕶indergarten 𝕲ifts and 𝕺ccupation 𝕸aterial.

𝕿he 𝕿hird 𝕲ift.

𝕱röbel's 𝕱irst 𝕭uilding 𝕭ox.

Large Cube, divided into eight small cubes of equal size. Aim: to illustrate form and number; also to give the first idea of fractions.

In Wooden Box,　　　　　　　　　　$0.30

Diagrams and **Directions** for using the Third Gift.

In Wrapper,　　　　　　　　　　$0.30

See also HOFFMANN, *Kindergarten Toys,* and other publications.

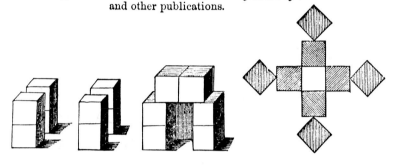

𝕿he 𝕱ourth 𝕲ift.

𝕱röbel's 𝕾econd 𝕭uilding 𝕭ox.

Large Cube, divided into eight oblong blocks. — The points of similarity and difference between this and the Third Gift should be indicated.

In Wooden Box,　　　　　　　　　　$0.30

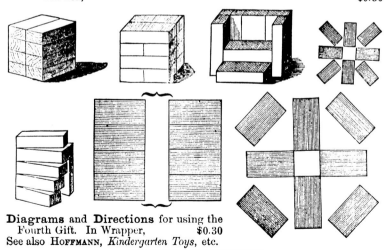

Diagrams and **Directions** for using the Fourth Gift. In Wrapper,　　　$0.30

See also HOFFMANN, *Kindergarten Toys,* etc.

E. Steiger, 22 & 24 Frankfort St., New York.

FIG. 3.　E. Steiger, *Kindergarten Gifts,* 1876. Third and Fourth Gifts.

The Fifth Gift.

Fröbel's Third Building Box.

This is a continuation of, and complement to, the **Third Gift**. It consists of twenty-one *whole,* six *half-,* and twelve *quarter-*cubes, forming altogether *one large Cube.*

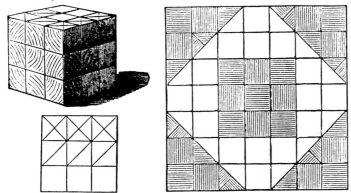

In Wooden Box, $0.75
Diagrams and **Directions** for using the Fifth Gift. In Wrapper, $0.60
See also HOFFMANN, *Kindergarten Toys,* etc.

The Fifth Gift B.

The Fifth Building Box (a combination of the Fifth and Second
Gifts). In Wooden Box, $1.00
Diagrams and **Directions** for using the Fifth Gift **B.** In Wrapper, $0.50

The Sixth Gift.

Fröbel's Fourth Building Box.

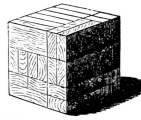

This is a continuation of, and complement to, the Fourth Gift. It consists of eighteen *whole* oblong blocks, three similar blocks divided lengthwise, and six divided breadthwise, forming altogether *one large Cube.*

In Wooden Box, $0.75

Diagrams and **Directions** for using the Sixth Gift. In Wrapper, $0.60

See also HOFFMANN, *Kindergarten Toys,* etc.

The Fifth Gift (FRŒBEL's Third Building Box), *extra-large size,*
1½ cubic feet. In strong Wooden Box, $7.20
The Sixth Gift (FRŒBEL's Fourth Building Box), *extra-large size,*
1½ cubic feet. In strong Wooden Box, $9.00

E. Steiger, 22 & 24 Frankfort St., New York.

FIG. 4.   E. Steiger, *Kindergarten Gifts,* 1876. Fifth and Sixth Gifts.

4   𝔎indergarten 𝔊ifts and 𝔒ccupation 𝔐aterial.

𝔗he 𝔖eventh 𝔊ift.

Quadrangular and triangular Tablets

of polished wood. These tablets, as well as the previous Gifts, are designed for instruction in reversing the position of forms and combining them. In the six previous Gifts the child had to do with *solids:* by the tablets the *plane* surfaces are represented; these are followed by the *straight line* in the Eighth Gift, and the *curve* in the Ninth Gift.

 A. Four large right-angled Triangles. In Wooden Box, $0.25

 B. Eight squares. In Wooden Box, $0.30
Diagrams to same. In Wrapper, $0.40

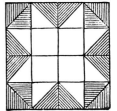

 C. Nine large equilateral Triangles. In Wooden Box, $0.30
Diagrams to same. In Wrapper, $0.40

 D. Sixteen isosceles Triangles. In Wooden Box, $0.30
Diagrams to same. In Wrapper, $0.40

E. Thirty-two isosceles Triangles. In Wooden Box, $0.40
Diagrams to same. In Wrapper, $0.40

F. Fifty - four equilateral Triangles. In Wooden Box, $0.50
Diagrams to same. In Wrapper, $0.40

G. Fifty-four isosceles Triangles. In Wooden Box, $0.50
Diagrams to same. In Wrapper, $0.40

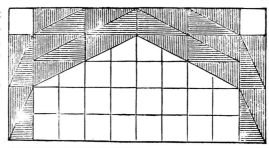 **H.** Fifty-six scalene Triangles. In Wooden Box, $0.60
Diagrams to same. In Wrapper, $0.40

FIG. 5.   E. Steiger, *Kindergarten Gifts*, 1876. Seventh Gift.

𝔎indergarten 𝔊ifts and 𝔒ccupation 𝔐aterial.   5

I. Sixty-four obtuse-angled Triangles.
In Wooden Box, $0.60
Diagrams to same. In Wrapper, $0.40

Box containing, in five divisions, Squares and the
four different kinds of Triangles (of binder's board),
with **Diagrams,** $1.60
Box with glass cover, containing, in five divisions,
Squares and the four different kinds of Triangles,
in finely colored and polished wood, $6.00

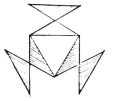

𝔗he 𝔈ighth 𝔊ift.

Sticks for Stick-laying. This
Gift consists of thin wooden Sticks,
about 13 inches long, to be cut into
various lengths by the teacher or
pupil, as occasion may require.
These Sticks, like most of the previous Gifts, are designed to teach
numerical proportions and forms.
Stick-laying is an excellent preparation for *drawing.* The Multiplica-
tion Table is *practically* taught by
means of this Gift. Reading, according to the *phonetic* method, is
taught by imitating with these
Sticks the letters of the Alphabet.
In the same way the Roman and
Arabic numerals are taught previous
to instruction in writing.

Package of 1000 Sticks, 1 inch
long, $0.30
Package of 1000 Sticks, 2 inches
long, $0.30
Package of 1000 Sticks, 3 inches
long, $0.30
Package of 1000 Sticks, 4 inches
long, $0.30
Package of 1000 Sticks, 5 inches
long, $0.30
Package of 500 Sticks, 13 inches
long, $0.50
Diagrams, in Wrapper, $0.30
Box with Sticks 1, 2, 3, 4, and 5
inches long, $0.35

Fröbel's Kindergarten Occupations for the Family. No. **1.** Stick-laying, $0.75

E. Steiger, 22 & 24 Frankfort St., New York.

FIG. 6.   E. Steiger, *Kindergarten Gifts,* 1876. Seventh Gift (continued) and Eighth Gift.

6   *Kindergarten Gifts and Occupation Material.*

The Ninth Gift.

Rings for Ring-laying. This Gift consists of whole and half Rings of *various sizes*, in wire, for forming figures. These Rings, like the Sticks in the Eighth Gift, are intended to teach the first elements of form as an introduction to *drawing*.

Box of whole and half Rings of various sizes, $0.75
Diagrams, in Wrapper, $0.60

The Tenth Gift.

Drawing on Slates and Paper. The material used is, first, *Slates* grooved in squares, next, *Paper* ruled in squares. This method of beginning drawing is the most systematic and perfect ever invented for young children. It is interesting to note how rapidly, by it, even the youngest pupils advance.

Slates, 13½ by 10 inches (No. 12), grooved in squares, ¼ inch wide, on one side, each $0.50
Slates, 12 by 9 inches (No. 9), grooved in squares, each $0.40
Slates, 10 by 7½ inches (No. 6), grooved in squares, each $0.30
Slates, 8½ by 6½ inches (No. 4), grooved in squares on one side, with narrow frame, rounded corners, each $0.30
Slate pencils (fine), per doz., $0.15, per gross, $1.50
Diagrams, in Wrapper, $0.30

E. Steiger, 22 & 24 Frankfort St., New York.

FIG. 7.   E. Steiger, *Kindergarten Gifts,* 1876. Ninth and Tenth Gifts.

Kindergarten Gifts and Occupation Material. 7

Drawing-Books, ruled in squares, ¼ inch wide, on both sides, each book containing 12 leaves, per doz., $0.79

Drawing-Books, ruled in squares, one-sixth inch wide, on both sides, per doz., $0.70

Paper ruled in squares, ¼ inch wide, on both sides, per quire (24 sheets), each 14 by 17 inches, $0.40

Paper ruled in squares, one-sixth inch wide, on both sides, per quire, $0.40

Pencils, per doz., $0.75

Pencils (fine), per doz., $0.90

K. FRŒBEL'S *Elements of Designing, on the Developing System, for Elementary School Classes, and for Families,* 4 Parts, each containing 24 pages ruled in squares, with designs and space for copying, each part $0.35

Part I. Straight Lines, and their Combinations.
Part II. Straight Lines, and their Combinations.
Part III. Straight Lines, and their Combinations.
Part IV. Circles and Curved Lines, and their Combinations.

Each page of the given examples is followed by a blank page for the Compositions, Combinations, or Inventions of the pupil.

Frœbel's Kindergarten Occupations for the Family. No. **2.** Drawing. $0.75

The Eleventh Gift.

Perforating (Pricking) Paper.

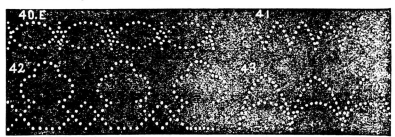

A Package of 50 leaves of paper, 11 by 8½ inches, ruled in squares *on one side only,* $0.50
Package of same, 25 leaves, $0.30

Perforating-Needles with long handles, per doz., $0.60
Perforating-Needles with short handles, per doz., $0.60
Perforating-Needles with long black handles, per doz., $0.25
Perforating-Cushions, each $0.25, per dozen, $2.40
Diagrams, in Wrapper $0.30

Frœbel's Kindergarten Occupations for the Family. No. **3.** Perforating. $0.75

E. Steiger, 22 & 24 Frankfort St., **New York.**

FIG. 8. E. Steiger, *Kindergarten Gifts,* 1876. Tenth Gift (continued) and Eleventh Gift.

𝕿he 𝕿welfth 𝕲ift.

Embroidering. The Perforating Material is also used in this Gift: after the pattern is perforated, it is embroidered with colored silk or worsted on card-board.

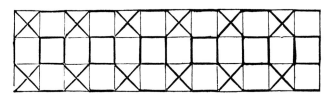

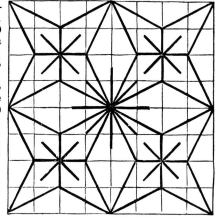

Material for perforating and embroidering, in Wrapper, Nos. 1, 2, 3, 4, each $0.50
Card-board ruled in squares *on one side*, Package of 25 leaves, $0.25
Blotting Pad, Package of 25, $0.15
Card-board (fine), Package of 25, $0.20
Twelve Designs, 8 by 6 inches, for perforating and embroidering, in Wrapper, Nos. 1 to 12, each $0.50
Card-board (fine), 8 by 6 inches, to be used with these Designs, Package of 12, $0.20
Twelve Designs, 5½ by 4 inches, for perforating and embroidering, in Wrapper, Nos. 1 to 6, each $0.35
Card-board (fine), 5½ by 4 inches, to be used with these Designs. Package of 12, $0.10
Card-board in sheets, 22 by 27 inches, in various colors, per sheet $0.10 or $0.12
Baskets for Cards or Needle-work, embossed, for perforating and embroidering in worsted or silk, and otherwise ornamenting and making up, 3 sizes, 7, 8, and 9 inches wide respectively. Package of 6, assorted, $0.50
Worsted Needles, per doz., in Wrapper, $0.15
Worsted, 12 assorted colors, with 3 Worsted Needles, in Wrapper, $0.25

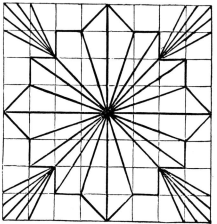

Embroidering Silk, 12 assorted colors, with 3 Needles, in Wrapper, $0.35

E. Steiger, 22 & 24 Frankfort St., New York.

FIG. 9.   E. Steiger, *Kindergarten Gifts*, 1876. Twelfth Gift.

The Thirteenth Gift.

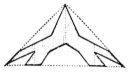

Cutting-Paper. Squares or Triangles of Paper are folded, cut according to certain rules, and formed into figures. The child's inclination for using the scissors is here so ingeniously turned to account as to produce very gratifying results.

Package of 100 squares, white, $0.20

Package of 100 squares colored, $0.20

Package of 100 squares, white and colored, mixed, $0.20

Diagrams to same, $0 75

Scissors, for Paper-Cutting, with rounded blades,   per pair $0.40

    per doz. $4.00

Package of 30 leaves, 9 inches square, of stout, ultramarine paper, for mounting the cut figures, $0.50

Package of 30 leaves, 9 inches square, of Manilla paper, $0.30

The Fourteenth Gift.

Weaving Paper. Strips of colored paper are, by means of a steel, brass, or wooden needle of peculiar construction, woven into another (differently colored) leaf of paper, which is cut into strips throughout its entire surface, except that a margin is left at each end to keep the strips in their places. A very great variety of designs is thus produced, and the inventive powers of teacher and pupil are constantly stimulated.

E. Steiger, 22 & 24 Frankfort St., New York.

FIG. 10.   E. Steiger, *Kindergarten Gifts*, 1876. Thirteenth and Fourteenth Gifts.

10   Kindergarten Gifts and Occupation Material.

Mats, 7 by 6 inches, with slits and corresponding strips for weaving, slits ⅛ inch wide (No. 1), Package of 1 doz., of various colors, $0.20

Mats, 7 inches square, slits ⅛ inch wide (No. 11), Package of 1 doz. $0.20

Mats, 7 by 6 inches, slits ¼ inch wide (No. 2), Package of 1 doz., $0.20

Mats, 7 inches square, slits ¼ inch wide (No. 12), Package of 1 doz., $0.20

Mats, 7 by 6 inches, slits 1-3 inch wide (No. 3), Package of 1 doz., $0.20

Mats, 7 inches square, slits 1-3 inch wide (No. 13), Package of 1 doz. $0.20

Mats, 7 by 6 inches, slits 1-6 inch wide (No. 4), Package of 1 doz., $0.20

Mats, 7 inches square, slits 1-6 inch wide (No. 14), Package of 1 doz , $0.20

Mats, 7 by 6 inches, slits 1-8 inch wide (No. 5), Package of 1 doz., $0.20

Mats, 7 inches square, slits 1-8 inch wide (No. 15), Package of 1 doz., $0.20

Mats, 7 by 6 inches, slits 1-12 inch wide (No. 6), Package of 1 doz., $0.20

E. Steiger, 22 & 24 Frankfort St., New York.

FIG. 11.   E. Steiger, *Kindergarten Gifts*, 1876. Fourteenth Gift (continued).

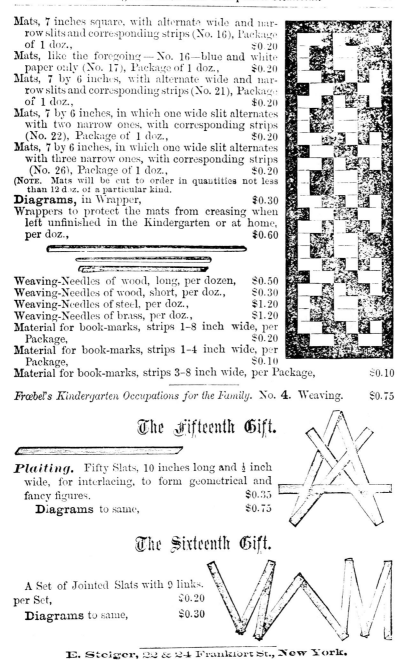

Mats, 7 inches square, with alternate wide and narrow slits and corresponding strips (No. 16), Package of 1 doz., $0.20

Mats, like the foregoing — No. 16—blue and white paper only (No. 17), Package of 1 doz., $0.20

Mats, 7 by 6 inches, with alternate wide and narrow slits and corresponding strips (No. 21), Package of 1 doz., $0.20

Mats, 7 by 6 inches, in which one wide slit alternates with two narrow ones, with corresponding strips (No. 22), Package of 1 doz., $0.20

Mats, 7 by 6 inches, in which one wide slit alternates with three narrow ones, with corresponding strips (No. 26), Package of 1 doz., $0.20

(NOTE. Mats will be cut to order in quantities not less than 12 doz. of a particular kind.

Diagrams, in Wrapper, $0.30

Wrappers to protect the mats from creasing when left unfinished in the Kindergarten or at home, per doz., $0.60

Weaving-Needles of wood, long, per dozen, $0.50
Weaving-Needles of wood, short, per doz., $0.30
Weaving-Needles of steel, per doz., $1.20
Weaving-Needles of brass, per doz., $1.20
Material for book-marks, strips 1–8 inch wide, per Package, $0.20
Material for book-marks, strips 1–4 inch wide, per Package, $0.10
Material for book-marks, strips 3–8 inch wide, per Package, $0.10

Frœbel's Kindergarten Occupations for the Family. No. **4**. Weaving. $0.75

The Fifteenth Gift.

Plaiting. Fifty Slats, 10 inches long and ½ inch wide, for interlacing, to form geometrical and fancy figures. $0.35

    Diagrams to same, $0.75

The Sixteenth Gift.

A Set of Jointed Slats with 9 links. per Set, $0.20

    Diagrams to same, $0.30

E. Steiger, 22 & 24 Frankfort St., New York.

FIG. 12.   E. Steiger, *Kindergarten Gifts,* 1876. Fourteenth Gift (continued), Fifteenth, and Sixteenth Gifts.

12   𝕶indergarten 𝕲ifts and 𝕺ccupation 𝕸aterial.

The Seventeenth Gift.

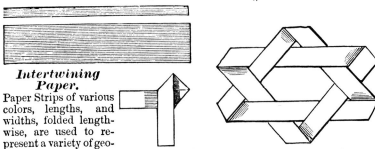

Intertwining Paper.

Paper Strips of various colors, lengths, and widths, folded length-wise, are used to re-present a variety of geo-metrical as well as fancy forms, by plaiting them according to certain rules.

Packages of Paper Strips of different length and width, containing 100 each, $0.20

Diagrams to same, $0.75

The Eighteenth Gift.

Folding Paper. The material for Paper-Folding consists of square, rectangular, and triangular pieces, with which variously shaped objects are formed, and the elements of geometry are taught in a practical man-ner. The variety is endless and prepares the pupil for many useful similar manual performances in practical life.

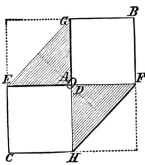

100 leaves, white, 4 inches square, $0.20
100 leaves, colored, 3½ inches square, $0.20
100 leaves, colored, 4 by 2 inches, $0.15
100 equilateral Triangles, white, sides
  6 inches long, $0.30
100 equilateral Triangles, colored, sides
  4 inches long, $0.25
Diagrams to same, $0.75

The Nineteenth Gift.

Peas or Cork Work. Peas are soaked in water for six or eight hours, and pieces of wire, of various lengths, pointed at the ends, are stuck into them for the purpose of imitating real objects and the various geometrical figures. Skeletons are thus pro-duced, which develop the eye for perspec e draw-ing most successfully. Sticks belonging to the Eighth Gift are also used for this purpose.

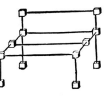

In place of Peas many persons prefer to use small Cork Cubes.
Wires of different lengths, per Package, $0.20
Cork Cubes, per Package of 100, $0.25
Diagrams to same, $0.75

E. Steiger, 22 & 24 Frankfort St., New York.

FIG. 13.   E. Steiger, *Kindergarten Gifts*, 1876. Seventeenth, Eighteenth, and Nineteenth Gifts.

The Twentieth Gift.

Modeling.　Bees-wax, Clay, Putty or other material, worked with a small wooden knife, on a light smooth board, is used for the purpose. These materials can be bought almost everywhere.

Modeling-Knives, of wood, each $0.10

Modeling-Knives, of wood, larger and better kind, each $0.20

Modeling-Boards of wood, each $0.12

Diagrams to same, $0.75

☞ Customers will please bear in mind that the method of describing Kindergarten Gifts, &c., in this Catalogue, is that adopted in America, which differs considerably from the one used in Germany and England. It is very important to remember this when ordering the Gifts &c. Only the first six Gifts are used in a strictly serial order, the Planes, Sticks, Weaving, and Embroidering materials being introduced at the same time as the Third Gift, so that the work of no two or three consecutive days need be alike. — The designation by numbers (No.) of various articles is entirely arbitrary, and is done solely for the purpose of enabling customers to *order* the exact kinds they desire to receive. — Requests to take back or exchange goods sent in conformity with orders must be declined.

Kindergarten Tables, 22 inches high, with cover of bass-wood (whitewood), marked off in squares one inch wide, nicely finished and varnished,

Tables, 30 inches wide, 6 feet long, $7.50

Tables, 30 inches wide, 9 feet long, $10.00

Tables for one child, each, 20 inches wide, 30 inches long, $3.00

Oil-cloth Covering, with light colored ground, one yard wide, marked off in squares one inch wide, supplied to order at $0.50 per running foot.

(This kind of covering may be used to fit ordinary tables temporarily for Kindergarten purposes.)

Kindergarten Chairs,　per dozen from $13.50 to $18.00

[Boxing and Shipping Expenses will be charged extra.]

Bust of Friedrich Frœbel, 8 inches high, with *Console,* $4.00

Photograph of Friedrich Frœbel, after a relief by O. MEYER, 8 by 9 inches, $3.00

The List on the foregoing pages comprises *only part of my Stock of Kindergarten Gifts, Occupation Material, etc.*

A very large assortment of kindred articles is on hand, and additions are incessantly made, both by importation from Europe and by domestic manufacture, so as to render mine **the most complete** and **most extensive Repository of the kind in America.**

To meet the growing demand, I offer, at a concession from regular prices, *Selections* —more or less complete—of *Kindergarten Gifts*

E. Steiger, 22 & 24 Frankfort St., New York.

FIG. 14.　E. Steiger, *Kindergarten Gifts,* 1876. Twentieth Gift.

of kindergarten publications for sale, some 230 of them, only 10 percent of them in English, the rest mostly in German. Contrary to my statement in the previous Note, one book by Friedrich Froebel was available in English by 1876, not a principal work, but *The Mother's Book of Song* with music composed by Lady Baker, selling for 75¢.

More puzzling than the Froebel box were some woodblock illustrations of Gothic churches on newsprint, yellowed and fragile, also preserved in the Wright Memorial Foundation files. FIG. 15. They recalled but did not correspond to a passage in *An Autobiography*. "Fascinated by buildings, she [Anna Wright] took ten full-page wood-engravings of the old English Cathedrals from 'Old England,' a pictorial publication to which the father had subscribed, had them framed simply in flat oak and hung upon the walls of the room that was to be her sons's. Before he was born, she said she intended him to be an architect."

Old England can refer only to a pictorial miscellany in two volumes, issued around 1845 in London by Charles Knight. But the full-page illustrations are dim chromolithographs and neither these nor the small black and white woodcuts could have served Anna Wright's purpose. Nor was there a periodical by that name which might be meant.

The woodcuts in the Taliesin West files suggest another possibility. They are either mounted, or consist of loose fragments. Two of them show legible signatures on their faces, "S. Read." Samuel Read is listed as an illustrator known for renderings of Gothic churches; his dates were 1816–1883. On the back of a badly stained fragment the following notice introduced a portion of narrative text, "[Begun in

Harper's Weekly No. 1203.]/A CONFIDENTIAL AGENT,/BY JAMES PAYN," and further fragments of text indicate that the cathedral pictured on the other side was Worcester. Thus it became possible to date the fragment to the issue of *Harper's Weekly* of 17 April 1881. This and similar illustrations were spread across two pages and accompanied by historical notes relating to each church. This practice seems to have begun in April of 1877 when York Cathedral was shown; then no further examples appear until September 1878. In December that year the illustrations began to be labeled "English Church Architecture," and in July of 1881 numbering was also introduced when Rochester Cathedral was noted as No. 16.

There are more puzzles. Why did dissenting parents, as Anna and William Wright certainly were, choose images of Church of England monuments to inspire their son? And what is indicated by the flat oak frames? In 1867 or even in 1881, the Arts and Crafts had no influence to exert; where did Anna Wright get the frames? Was the architect perhaps imposing his taste unconsciously on his recollections? In his earlier works flat oak strips played an important role.

A final note. Whatever the decoration of the Wright nursery may have been, the surviving prints in the files come from the late 1870s and earlier 1880s. It was in 1878 that the Wrights moved back to the Middle West, to Madison, Wisconsin. Summers young Frank worked for his uncles and aunts near Spring Green, but winters he went to school in Madison; it might have seemed an opportune moment to direct his attention toward architecture.

I am grateful to the Frank Lloyd Wright Memorial Foundation for permission to publish the illustrations they generously provided.

FIG. 15.   Samuel Read, Worcester Cathedral, *Harper's Weekly,* 17 April 1881.

FIG. 16. Adler and Sullivan, the Auditorium Building, Chicago, 1887–90.

Frank Lloyd Wright's 'Lieber Meister'

When Frank Lloyd Wright, in his twentieth year, decided against the advice of his elders to seek a career as architect in the great city of Chicago, he worked first for J. Lyman Silsbee (whom he had come to know not long before as the designer of a chapel for Wright's kindred near Spring Green, Wisconsin). Although at Silsbee's he quickly became a competent renderer, as published images show, he was not impressed by the architectural quality of the projects he worked on, he says in *An Autobiography*. Seeking more guidance and better pay he moved to the office of W.W. Clay, then working without partners and with a small staff. Wright, with brief training in drafting and (at the University of Wisconsin) in the rudiments of engineering, found himself faced with problems of architectural design beyond his competence. Then he returned to Silsbee — at a better rate of pay — but continued to look for a more inspiring master.

The young engineer, Paul Mueller, a recent immigrant from Germany, had moved from Silsbee's office to that of Adler and Sullivan who were hiring hands to help with their important new assignment, the Auditorium Building on Michigan Avenue. FIG. 16. Mueller suggested that Wright might fit into this promising situation, and Wright was interviewed by Louis H. Sullivan. FIG. 17. It was the beginning of a fundamental awakening of Wright's abilities and ideas. Wright became Sullivan's close assistant, and Sullivan became Wright's 'Lieber Meister.'

What were the basic influences of Sullivan on Wright? Sullivan was not only a designer of buildings but a man to whom architecture was more than a business, or even a profession, but rather a fundamental component in the development of human society. In fact, the aims and means of architecture were changing in accord with a reunited and rapidly industrializing nation. Sullivan had only recently become a full partner of Dankmar Adler, an experienced engineer, highly reputed. FIG. 18. Sullivan had sought an education as professional architect, aware of the aesthetic impact of great buildings, and he was an avid reader of texts which might illuminate the art. But he was equally enthusiastic about the daring work of bridge builders opening up vast expanses of the continent, and of a different set of engineers transforming the

FIG. 17.   Louis H. Sullivan, around 1890.

FIG. 18.   Dankmar Adler, around 1890.

roots of buildings so that ever greater loads might be supported safely and economically. Thus Sullivan complemented Adler's special abilities while he was in full sympathy with them.

Paul Mueller soon became close to Adler, as Wright was to Sullivan. Inevitably the two young men (who were to work together off and on for almost half a century, long after Adler and Sullivan separated) were well acquainted with the ideas of Frederick Baumann and others who followed him in changing and improving the substructures of buildings. FIG. 19. The craft of fireproofing; the shift from iron, cast or wrought, to steel; the gradual but steady

enlargement of glazed windows, which led to perimeter heating; the progress of mechanical elevators, almost as essential as the great bridges; and not least, a nascent realization of the potentials of cantilevering — all these revolutionary trends required rethinking the art of architecture, as Sullivan, Wright, and Mueller realized.

If the magnitude and vitality of this situation are borne in mind, then two of Sullivan's legacies to Wright, so often misunderstood or scorned as moonshine, become more comprehensible. I mean those two words they applied to architecture: *organic* and *democratic*.

The great tradition of architecture which

THE ART OF PREPARING

FOUNDATIONS

FOR ALL KINDS OF BUILDINGS,

WITH PARTICULAR ILLUSTRATION OF THE

"METHOD OF ISOLATED PIERS,"

AS FOLLOWED IN CHICAGO.

BY

FREDERICK BAUMANN,

Architect.

WITH NINETEEN WOODCUTS.

CHICAGO:
J. M. WING & CO., PUBLISHERS.
1873.

FIG. 19.   Frederic Baumann's chief publication, 1873.

had spread over many centuries from the Euphrates to the Thames was being superseded, not without contest, by a new insight that arose beside the Seine and soon flourished in industrializing America. Democracy was taking unanticipated forms and an appropriate architecture gradually grew with it, organically part of it, utilizing technologies and structural innovations developed in the untrammeled, individualistic society of the New World. In this sense *democratic* and *organic* were synonyms.

The old, entrenched expressions with their curious tribal names — Doric, Ionic, Roman, Gothic — had been 'revived' more than once, but the sap of life flowed elsewhere. To bring a new architecture to fruition was no small ambition, and the 'New School of the Middle West,' as Wright called it, took errant paths, was somewhat insecure, but its aims were clear especially to Sullivan and Wright. The unique reputation of Wright, today worldwide, is based on this inner vision which he inherited and boldly advanced over a long career, searching for forms of architecture organically congruent with the evolving American way of life.

Thus Wright owed to his apprenticeship under Sullivan an architectural ideal and an acquaintance with the new means of achieving it; 'Lieber Meister' was no empty title.

Nevertheless 'Lieber Meister' poses a question; why a German locution when 'Cher Maître' or some other would have been equally likely? German culture had long been part of the Chicago scene; in 1871 when the great fire occurred, and when in Europe the Germans had vanquished France, a street in Chicago was named Goethe Street. Though Wright's heritage was predominantly Welsh and English, Sullivan's maternal grandparents who took

FIG. 20.   Adler and Sullivan, the Schiller Theater, Chicago, 1891–92.

care of him during much of his childhood were German and Swiss. It is not certain that Sullivan understood German; an English translation of *Faust* and a set of Goethe's works in German were among his books. But Adler, contrariwise, spent his first ten years in Germany and had close connections with the German Jewish community in Chicago. When Wright joined the Adler and Sullivan office he became involved with several commissions for this group, not

FIG. 21. Goethe Monument, donated by the Germans of Chicago, placed at an entry to Lincoln Park, 1913.

only residences but club embellishments and a synagogue. Moreover, one of the firm's major structures, the Schiller Building, was made to serve a separate segment of the German population; German plays were staged there and a German club had large quarters in the tall building behind the tower. FIG. 20. German groups in America were exhorted to present German culture publicly, and a competition was held in the motherland for monuments to Goethe which might be erected. The club in the Schiller Building probably was involved in this effort, for, after nearly fifty thousand dollars had been raised in Chicago, the winning design of the competition was set up at an entrance to Lincoln Park, a colossal male figure with a sharp-looking eagle on its knee. FIG. 21. It is still to be seen, in good repair after some damage by lightning. But more than these links to Germany, it must have been the day-to-day association with Paul Mueller and the other Germans in the Adler and Sullivan office, augmented by Sullivan's high regard for John Edelmann, a peripatetic socialist of German-Jewish extraction, that led to the choice of a German honorific for the architect who molded much of Wright's ideas and skills. Despite all their differences, Sullivan was acknowledged by Wright as his legitimate professional parent. To understand Wright's code of architectural principles one must consider Sullivan's own, only partly explicit ideas. And to understand why the Harvard professor Kuno Francke probably recommended Wright to the Berlin publishers Ernst Wasmuth, one may assume that Francke was informed about the German element in the culture of Chicago and its architectural ramifications. Thus Wright's great double portfolio which gave him authority in the minds of younger European architects may have owed a good deal to 'Lieber Meister.'

I am especially grateful to Timothy Samuelson of the commission on Chicago Architectural Monuments for illustrations, advice, and discussion, and I thank John Vinci for directing me to him. I am grateful to Ronald Krueck of Krueck and Olsen, Chicago, for authorizing Kit Krankel to research the stories on Goethe Street and the Goethe monument. Mr. Samuelson gave me a copy of Paul Mueller's testimony in court, dated 1925 and appended below, which so well evokes the character of the Adler and Sullivan office when Wright joined it. At the library of the Art Institute of Chicago Mary Woolever discovered that the document came to them for microfilming from Vern O. McClurg, a lawyer since deceased whose professional interests devolved on the firm of Jansen and Halstead. They graciously allowed its use here. Bruce Pfeiffer, the Archivist of the Frank Lloyd Wright Memorial Foundation, has kindly, as ever, permitted me to reproduce his letter telling of Olgivanna Lloyd Wright's recollections of Paul Mueller when he was working with Wright on the project for San Marcos in the Desert. Goethe references will be found in Chicago newspapers: *Tribune*, 18 September 1910, 22 September 1913, 23 March 1914, 15 September 1951, and 3 May 1981; *Sun Times*, 15 January 1940, 12 December 1985; *Daily News*, 8 July 1954.

October 1925

TESTIMONY OF PAUL F. P. MUELLER, testified in Court*

I live at 1445 Granville Avenue, Chicago. I am a contractor and builder. I left the profession of architecture some thirty odd years ago. I did not receive a technical training in architecture. I went through the government school of mining and civil engineering in the Saar Basin, Germany, and I passed my examination for the polytechnic, but came to Chicago in 1881. I went to work here with various architects and draftmen; was engaged by the Aetna Iron Company, Clark, Raffner & Company, and S.S. Wetner, engineers; also superintended the erection of steel structures. At present I am engaged by the Continental & Commercial National Bank to look after their interests in the construction of the Morrison Hotel. After I was with the Aetna Iron Works, Mr. Adler engaged me to work on the steel construction of the Auditorium Building. Well, we had, of course, all the buildings that Adler & Sullivan built in those days. I was in their office for seven years, had charge of their office, and when I was in six weeks, Mr. Adler turned the office over to me as foreman. Instead of being the designing engineer I became foreman of the whole office. There was the Standard Club and, of course, a great many manufacturing buildings that we built in those days. There was the McVickers Building, remodeling the Hooley Building, consultations about Carnegie Hall in New York, in connection with Mr. Tunnihill, the

* Mueller's testimony is printed here exactly as shown in the court record of United States Circuit Court of Appeals for the Seventh Circuit, October term, 1925, no., 3733, Chicago Auditorium Association vs. Mark Skinner Willing and the Northern Trust Co., as Trustees, p. 448.

architect, remodeling of the Pabst Theatre in Milwaukee, the Pueblo Opera House in Pueblo; plans for the hotel in Salt Lake City; and there was the Kleiber Building on Wabash Avenue. We had the contract for the Schiller Building. I was secretary and consulting engineer of the Probst Construction Company, which had many of the buildings at the World's Fair. I have had experience in connection with many buildings in the City of Chicago. I was called on to go to Japan and built the Imperial Hotel there about six years ago. I built St. Paul's Roman Catholic Church in Chicago for Mr. Schlack. That church is built with masonry walls, Gothic architecture, without any steel or other reinforcing. At the Holy Name Cathedral, I cut into the apse and moved it 150 feet to the rear and put new foundations under it, and there was new foundations put under the tower. The tower leaned about 13 inches into the street, and there was caissons put under the tower. I don't know exactly how high those towers are, maybe 120 or 130 feet. They are of masonry construction. I think it was the year 1883 that I first went with Adler & Sullivan. The first thing I did with them was to start on the diagrams for the Auditorium Building. I was first engaged as engineer and then afterwards I was put in charge of the office. I was with them for seven years. We had about between 30 and 40 draftsmen. We had a number of construction engineers. There was Mr. North, who is at present chief editor of American Architecture. He made out a design of these stresses. Then there was Mr. Angus, an engineer was has been for thirty years with the Chicago Building Department, as designing engineer. Then there was Mr. Strobel, as consulting engineer, and Mr. Marburg, who made the drawings of the stress and theatre part of the building. These men worked on various works and, of course, my time was mostly taken up in making drawings of the engineer and architects and draftsmen working harmony. And they had a number of other engineers, like the Sanitary engineers, and stage engineers. Mr. Adler was very apt to have almost an expert for every branch of the building that was built. Mr. Adler himself was active in the supervision of these matters. He himself was an engineer. He had been through the technical school in Detroit, and then he volunteered for the army in the Civil War, and was soon after that appointed to the Engineering Corps, which he served on through the Civil War, and he also at that time made the acquaintance of Mr. Colonel Sooy Smith, who, at the time of the Auditorium Building, was consulting engineer for the foundations and other matters. We all knew these men were reputed as being the best men he could get hold of. As far as I could see, Mr. Adler did all he possibly could to get the best men for every particular line of work. Then the question of stage machinery came up, he took a trip to Europe and took the stage manager of the Auditorium along, to get the stage machinery which was at that time available after the Ring Theatre fire in Vienna. He brought those plans back and they were worked over to American mechanism, and for that effect he engaged Mr. Herman, who was reputed as one of the best elevator machinery engineers, and he worked with me on the drawings to get the stage machinery working. The lay-out of the kitchen arrangement for the hotel, when that was to be made, Mr.

Southgate sent his chief steward from New York, and that was all laid out according to their plans. In all these matters Mr. Adler usually consulted the people who wanted to use it, and made an effort to make it the most satisfactory that could be done. There was not one general contract for the building; it was let separately. The steel construction was Smead Iron Company in Louisville, and before he would award that contract to them he sent me to Louisville to see what their facilities were and what their reputation was. Mr. Adler sent me down there. The steel was let to the Carnegie Steel Company. At that time they had just opened their steel hearth in Homestead Mills, and the trusses and part of the theatre was let to the Keystone Bridge Company, of which Mr. Strobel was consulting Engineer, and he was very often in the office consulting Mr. Adler. The shop drawings were made by Mr. Marburg, who afterwards became Professor of Civil Engineering of the University of Pennsylvania. Mr. Osborne and Mr. Lichter, they are the sanitary engineers. The steel men, of course, they were the best in the country, and the masonry work was let to Mr. Angus, who, of course, had a very high reputation; and Mr. Lichter, who testified here, had a very high reputation. He was a good man when I saw him working on this building I made up my mind when I would go into business he would be my partner, and so it happened Mr. Lichter became my partner afterwards. The granite work was let to Hinsdale, who was very well reputed, at least. The stonework was by Reed, one of the best stone men we had in the City of Chicago at the time; and the setting of the steel was let to McGuire, and the fireproofing was let to the Illinois Terra Cotta Lumber Company. That was porous terra cotta. It was mixed with sawdust and burned, and in burning the sawdust out, it would leave the terra cotta porous, which would leave it much lighter, and was considered fireproof. In connection with this fireproofing, Mr. Adler had consulted Mr. P.B. White, who was one of the originators of the fireproofing, and Eiger & Beidler, of this Terra Cotta Lumber Company. I knew Ferdinand Peck by sight. He was very often in the office. In fact, quite often I complained that there were too many conventions in the office, on account of the draftsmen did not do enough work. They couldn't do work fast enough. He was constantly in touch with Mr. Adler, and even when it came to the layout of the theatre he consulted Mr. Daly, at that time a very noted stage theatre man. Mr. Adler had men in Pittsburgh who reported to him on the progress in Pittsburgh, and once or twice he made a personal visit to Pittsburgh, to see that material before it would come on. The superintendence of the building was in the hands of Capt. Neiman, an experienced builder, in the employ of Martin A. Ryerson, and he was engaged by the Association to be there continuously on the premises, to see that the work was carried on properly. He was employed by the Association direct. Prior to that he had been with Martin A. Ryerson. These various plans went through my hands before they were completed. There was so many drawings of the Auditorium made of it that they spent nearly all their commissions making drawings. They spent nearly $60,000 making plans for the Auditorium. There was a complete set of plans for the building. In the preparation of the plans and specifications of the materials that went into the building, the Chicago Building Code then in force and effect was consulted. Of course, there was a good many things came up that the Chicago Building Code used at that time did not cover. And then Mr. Adler would consult the officials, and sometimes we would have to wait until a certain decision would be given. We also had in the preparation of these plans, the tables and formulae that had been compiled by authorities who were leaders in their field at the time, and Mr. Adler insisted on using the formulae that were laid down in the handbook on engineering, and we used 156,000 pounds of stress on the steel and 12,000 on the cast iron, or course, modified carefully according to the loading and so forth.

Generey Sooy Smith was consulted as to the foundations, and they put testing tanks upon the premises, and loaded it and watched it, and finally loaded it heavier until it sank, and they arrived at the figure, and they told me to figure two and one-quarter tons on the square foot for all the foundations, and then the weights were all tabulated and put in a book, and all the steel columns were recorded in a book, and Mr. Adler would check those up. I knew at one time I spent six weeks at Mr. Adler's house, and every night we would go over the matters that came up during the day, and he would check it up in his own house before he would tell us to go ahead. The men were all educated engineers that worked on it, and afterwards they became noted engineers; some of them. Mr. Adler died, I think, in 1900. Mr. Sullivan, of Adler & Sullivan, died some few years ago, while I was in Japan. Mr. Probst died, too, I think, while I was away. I had a set of the plans of the Auditorium. I am very sorry they were burned up. Mrs. Mueller burned them up ten or twelve years ago. When I left Adler & Sullivan and went into the building business, I was interested in the settlement that was going on in the Auditorium at the time I was still with Adler & Sullivan, and then I was engaged to put in lintels with iron brackets to support them. I am familiar with the construction of the building, as I remember it from the time it was designed and put up, and as my memory has been refreshed by recent visits. I heard Mr. Lichter describe the foundations. I consider the description that he gave of it substantially correct. The grillage under the walls, and everywhere except under the tower particularly, went down about four feet below city datum, and under the tower, I think, one foot more. That was necessary to keep the timbers continuously immersed in water. The wooden grillage under the outside walls is practically on the same level as the bottom of the piers through the building. The tower was lower, because we needed the timbar to make the offset. The sand mentioned by Mr. Lichter as being under the grillage was put there, I think, for leveling it, and I think for giving the water a chance to be conveyed there and be on the bottom of the timbers. I think, there was crushed stone all around this to facilitate the conveying of water around the timbers. Water will not ordinarily permeate through clay. Most of the clay we have here in the City of Chicago is water tight. Rubble masonry is masonry that has no particular size to it. Plaintiff's Exhibit 51 shows rubble foundations under the column. Some people call it bridge masonry. It could not be compared with our ordinary Chicago rubble masonry. That is a typical portion of the construction of the tower. The piers of the front wall are dimension stone. The bearing capacity of dimension stone as compared with stone that is not dimension stone in the building, or rubble masonry, is a great deal better. You can load a great deal more load on it. In the ordinary rough rubble masonry there may be round or irregular-shaped stones. They are supposed to bond them and the mortar helps them. Of course, ordinary common rubble masonry is not as efficient as the masonry used in the Auditorium Building as to weight carrying capacity. There is not very much mortar in this dimension stone masonry; the beds are fairly level. The dimension stone masonry was used in bridge construction until the concrete came in use. Concrete can be made much more economically and in combination with steel is used more than that now. Except where they do use concrete on bridges, this dimension stone, such as is used on the Auditorium, and just identified by the photographs, is the kind they use.

I looked at Plaintiff's Exhibits 76 and 77, which were produced and identified as samples of stone, mortar, and cement taken from the building, at the same time they were offered in evidence, and have looked at both those exhibits again just now. The mortar shows that it is just as strong, if not stronger, than either the brick or stone that was in connection with it. If it was poor mortar, it would come off freely. As to the fact that the mortar has clung to the brick, so that in chipping out the mortar a piece of the brick came with it, I think the Auditorium walls are about as good walls as we have here in the City of Chicago. Selected brick went into those walls. I have not seen any soft brick. We had an old hand at the inspection. If he spied any soft brick he would not allow it to go in. In going around the building lately I haven't seen any brick that was weathered at all anywhere.

The interior columns were of cast iron, and the beams and girders were of steel, and the trusses also steel. So far as I know all the structural members of that building that are metal, with the exception of the columns, are steel, because they came from the Homestead Mill, which at that time had been turned over to Bessemer steel production, and the years after that nearly all the mills in the east followed the suit of the Carnegie mill, in changing from wrought iron mills into steel mills. That is just my inference. I never examined as to that fact myself. I didn't examine the steel, only I know that it came from the mill, and the mill had been changed into Bessemer steel manufacture. I had nothing to do with the placing of the order of the metal work, any more than Mr. Adler sent me down there to see whether the Smead Iron Works was able to carry out the work. They had the general contract for the steel, and steel was made at the Carnegie Steel Company, through the Snead Iron Works, and the Snead Iron Works made all the iron castings. They were cast in Louisville and set up here. At the time of the drawing of the plans for the columns, we used the then best known engineering formulae in determining the size of those columns; they were all checked and rechecked by the different engineers. When we sent the drawings out into the shop, there were again shop drawings made under Mr. Strobel, and Mr. Marburg of the trusses, and they changed somewhat the details we had made, because they used the shapes and the numbers that best fitted to their shop methods, and all these drawings were redrawn. They had the strain diagrams and the load given to them and before they would put any work in Mr. Adler again checked them and put his name on them. He was an engineer himself. The plans did not call for water to be in any of the columns. Of course, in erecting the column, the column is open on top, and, of course, it can rain into it. I don't know of any other water that can get into there. In the preparation of the plans for the building, there was consideration to settlement given. The exact number of inches or feet was not given, nor any unit of measurement as to how much it would settle. We did not make an exact allowance on it, but from experience Mr. Adler told me it might settle four or even more inches, and we had put in some screws in the bottom of all the light columns, under the sidewalk as well as under the center of the first floor of the hotel. They were put under the columns with a thread, so that they could be screwed out, and if I remember, they were six inches long, so that you could screw them six inches. Those were the sidewalk columns, all light columns.

As regards balancing the live load and dead load, the structure, the ten story structure, was figured with 90 per cent in the top story, and reduced by 10 per cent as we went down, so in reality we had about 50 per cent of all the live load figured on the outside walls. On the interior of the theatre we had a little less than one-half, but it was still too much. And, furthermore, we figured the public parts of the building. It took some time for Mr. Adler, before he informed us what we could use, and he finally told me to use 75 pounds for all the public rooms for the live load, while in the hotel and office building 50 pounds was used. Now, that resulted in a heavier live load on the columns on the interior of the Auditorium than there ought to have been there, and that was one of the things Mr. Adler was always sorry about, and in after years he watched the building, and said to his regret that the rest of it went down and the inside of the theatre stood, and he, of course, was very careful that anything that would wrench or crack he would change and rectify; and about two months before he died he called me down to see whether I would not be willing to take a contract to cut the columns off — that is, in the auditorium only — cut them off, each one of them, as much as they stood up, and lower them down so as to make the auditorium floor level again. But, of course, he died shortly afterwards and I paid no more attention to that. Now, that auditorium stayed up on account of too much live load being allowed on the foundations, and the foundations being small, the circumference of the piers has more shoring in the ground than the rest of it. About everything else, on Wabash Avenue and on Congress Street and on Michigan Avenue, the interior columns have hardly any perceptible difference between the outside walls. I have lately gone through the building from top to bottom, everywhere, and can hardly find any great variations in the levels in the floors in the outer portion of the Auditorium Building; I mean in the hotel or office building; while, of course, the Auditorium has that settlement across the foyers, and of course it is visible to everybody, and the last time I heard of the levels taken it was about 20 inches. The settlement of the outside walls of the building has been fairly uniform, although the extreme from one year, from the highest year to the lowest, is about eight inches while the adjoining piers is nowhere more than three inches, while in the auditorium that is entirely different. In the auditorium the settlement was much more. I dare say the first row of columns to the heavy brick walls is as much as a foot, if not more, in the levels, and that is where the brackets and the struts were broken, on account of the additional strain that was put on them through this settlement of the heavy walls.

We figured this heavy live load, principally on the interior foundations for the columns that were to be inside the theatre. Those are the ones that are still up. Take, for instance, an auditorium having 4,000 seats, and take the weight of 4,000 people on that foundation with the square area we have there, it doesn't even come to 40 pounds if it was filled continuously.

Those jacks were put under the sidewalk columns and the columns supporting the first floor on Congress Street. There is no interior columns going to the top of the building except on the northern part of Wabash Avenue, the two columns in the tower and then the columns on Michigan Avenue. Congress Street has no interior columns except in the basement supporting the first floor. These columns that appear on Plaintiff's Exhibit 57, which were testified to having jacks under them would be the columns in the basement under the first floor along Congress Street. The load on these columns is just that one floor. There are no columns that go higher, setting on top of these and going right on up. There isn't enough load on that. For that reason they put these jack screws on the bottom. The span on the second floor is taken care of by the girders running from the auditorium wall to the front wall. As to the span on each side of the column shown in this picture, that column with the jack under it is adequate to support that one floor. The columns under the sidewalk on that support are about 8 feet. In those days they used the cast iron members. Every 8 feet is one of these little columns. This column on Plaintiff's Exhibit 57 could be taken out without endangering the structure of the building, the roof shored up and another column put in there, but why should the column be taken out? It could be done. You would have to shore up the weight of only one floor. It isn't necessary to do that now. They can fireproof that column.

After the building was designed, there were some alterations in the construction or plans made whereby additional dead loads were put on the building. I am sorry to say that Adler & Sullivan were so solicitous of the opinions of others. They consulted Professor Ware as to the design, consulted professional men of all kinds, when working on the drawings. Professor Ware was Professor of Architecture in the School of Technology in Boston. He was called in to criticize the drawings, particularly two sets of drawings. One set was very ornate, made for terra cotta, very light, projecting bay windows, with iron columns from the second floor. It was all designed in detail. They then considered that was too frivolous or ornate, should be more of a monumental character. Then the design of stone was submitted to Professor Ware. He criticized the proportions of the tower and added two stories to the tower after the bottom course of the tower foundation was already in. We changed the brick walls into hollow brick in order to reduce that additional weight, but the mortar going into the hollows of the hollow brick didn't quite make it up. We put in the heaviest beams we could get then, 20 inches I think, extending them to the adjoining piers, front and rear. The object was to carry and spread the additional pressure that would be on the tower onto the adjoining piers and not make that settlement abrupt. I believe if those beams had not been put in the tower would have shown a separation from the rest of the walls to such an extent it would have been alarming, like the tower of the Board of Trade. The Board of Trade tower was leaning out and separated from the rest of the walls so that it was ordered taken down by the City of Chicago. In the Auditorium that was prevented by having these beams and thereby spreading the load. In the early years after the building was put up the settlement in the tower was more than it is now. You could see it on the third story and on the sidewalk. By the late measurements of the settlements I know it has equalized itself more than years ago when I was familiar with it. I was away for a number of years in Japan.

After the construction was started, Mr. Southgate said he needed a banquet floor. The banquet hall was designed to go over the roof. It was projected after the footings were in. The additional load of the banquet hall, coming on the north wall, and the inside wall of the theatre, aggravated the heavier walls, and was also one of the reasons these walls went down more than on the inside of the theatre. Besides that, they decided a prominent building which at that time had already got notoriety, had to have a large organ. So they designed it. But they had no room for it. We had to cut out a piece out of the north wall and project the floor out over the alley, and that whole organ chamber was hung with steel rods up to the bottom of those trusses, so as to keep the weight on the Auditorium Building and not on the Studebaker Building. I have not seen the bench mark, testified to by the witness A'Neals, but from his description I understood that the bench mark was in a straight line south from the rear wall of the Studebaker Building. That would bring it practically where this organ chamber was added. Then there were additions made to the dressing rooms over this alley east of the organ chamber. That was done some years after the entire building was completed. Then above these dressing rooms there was an extension of the Studebaker Building over onto the Auditorium Building. So, naturally, there is different loads coming up that were originally entirely unknown. The portion of the front of the hotel which hitches onto the Studebaker Building was put on cantilever foundations so as not to touch the Studebaker Building footings. The addition of the organ loft and dressing rooms, and the other various additions which are part of the Fine Arts Building or tower, added to the dead load on the foundations of the wall at these particular points. That is the only reason I could see why there should be additional settlement at Mr. A'Neals bench mark for the last five years while all the rest of the building has practically stood dormant as far as settlement is concerned. The recital hall was in the original design. These various additions to the original design added decidedly to the dead weight of the structure on the foundation walls. They did not add weight on the structural members of the building such as the columns; almost entirely on the brick walls.

The walls surrounding the stage are continuous; nearly all the brick walls surrounding the building are continuous walls except the proscenium opening. In the middle of the stage the floor is entirely on hydraulic jacks. It floats on water contained in the cylinders. They are constructed after the patents of the Asphilia Iron Company of Vienna. Asphilia is a Greek word referring to the safety of foundation construction. There are only three threatres in the world today that can compare with the stage machinery of the Auditorium as to this method. In order to get that system into the ground, sinking of the stage floor 18 feet, there is a displacement there of 36 feet, and that had to be dug into the ground. While they were digging those 28 cisterns, we had a settlement around the outside tower wall of almost four inches during the six weeks while these cisterns were being put in. They were put in by Sooy Smith. Whether these methods were as efficient as nowadays, I don't know. Outside of the cylinders, and the squeezing in of the ground caused really the first settlement of the Auditorium. That was around the foundation. That took place before the building was up. It was really the first warning that we had softer ground to stand on that Mr. Adler originally thought. The stage machinery is entirely contained on these cylinders, where the beams go on the heavy brick walls, the whole floor is supported on the pistons. The beams where they into the wall were, of course, bent down in connection with the settlement. The Auditorium Association has released those beams and raised them up where they were in the wall. They have bolted new brackets on to make it level. I suppose the Auditorium Association did that work. I do not know anything about it, except I saw those brackets put on the columns. I have seen those brackets; who put them on I don't know. These pistons still work. I have seen them working there a few weeks ago. They operated so as to raise and lower the stage. I don't think they could get out of alignment. They stick 28 or 30 feet into the ground.

There are two stage curtains. The inner curtain is for ordinary performances, ordinary stage width. Then there is a larger curtain for spectacular purposes, balls and concerts, 75 foot opening, decorated with plaster, and it weighs about 11 tons. That curtain is used. I saw it dipped day before yesterday. It still works.

The tower is on one big footing, bigger than this room, I think, all in one. The whole tower, interior columns and everything, sets on that raft, three layers of timbers, concrete and rails, and on top of it is the masonry. The beams are on either side into those piers. At the time it was built Mr. Adler was afraid this big footing of the tower would not have enough weight to press on the ground and the rest of the building would get its weight and settle, so pig iron and bricks were put on, almost the total amount of bricks that were necessary for the tower. The bricks would then be used from the pile as it went up. That was in order to give the ground under the tower the benefit of the squeeze. That was all in anticipation that there would be a settlement.

In the outside walls on Michigan Avenue and Congress that granite in the second floor is the whole thickness as the piers. The walls above are Bedford stone with brick backing. Practically half of the pier is stone. That is true, generally speaking, all the way over the whole Auditorium. It was not made in the modern method of veneering stone on brick walls. The average is more than six inches for the facing. I would say about one-half the area of the piers is stone. The windows come fairly well in. The piers come back. The stone mullions in the arched openings between the window piers on Michigan Avenue go down to the third floor. On the third floor there are beams which carry the mullions, and the mullions themselves carry the floor that goes on them. In Defendant's Exhibits 6 and 8, which are pictures of the Michigan Avenue front and the Congress Street front of the building, it is these mullions, these stone piers in the middle of this big arch here [indicating]. On Michigan Avenue, instead of these mullions being carried by that pier, that mullion goes all the way down here, under this floor are heavy beams, they carry all this work, the pier has only itself to carry. The granite lintels on the second floor were, of course, considered too long, and were bolted through with nuts on the bottom, through these cast iron beams. They are hung on the iron and do not support themselves. These granite columns on Michigan Avenue are supported on a keystone with those in the arch. Mr. Sullivan did not want to have any chance of that stone being cracked, so the columns were drilled and a bolt put in and those columns are hanging on steel cantilevers. A calculation of the stress in the piers on the Michigan Avenue front would not be accurate unless it took into consideration the load carried by the mullion columns.

When we calculated the stress on the banquet hall floor, we used only 75 pounds through all the public rooms. It took quite a while before Mr. Adler gave us orders to use 75 pounds. The standard used in those days was just a question of how much load we could get on it. If people get as close together as they can, they cannot make any more than 75 pounds. That was not any prescribed amount in the city code. We had to figure it out. If people stand close together they do not weigh more than 75 pounds. In a banquet hall you can't get anything like it unless there happens to be a panic. The average auditorium gives fully ten feet or more to each person, either in the theatre or in the banquet hall. A man would occupy about 4 or 4½ square feet of space sitting down in the seat, but there are the aisles and so on. If he weighs 200 pounds that would make a live load per foot of about 40 pounds. The ordinance now for a banquet hall live load is 100 pounds. That was not in force when we made these calculations for the Auditorium; that was a later edition. Naturally. I watched it every time I went to the Auditorium with Mr. Thielbar and Mr. Renwick to see what the condition of the building was, in reference to settlement and anything that would appear as necessary. Last week I went over the office building as well as the hotel, from the top clear down to the bottom, everywhere I could get into a room or get an excuse for looking in, to look for any beam deflected enough to show cracks in the plaster. I have not been able to find a single place a beam was deflected in either the office building or the hotel building to such an extent that the plaster would crack under it. Even in the Auditorium Building where these props have been replaced, all the beams I could see, I sighted to the bottom of them, and I could not find a single deflected em. The long girders on the second floor show a deflection, but not enough to crack the plaster. I did not see any broken brackets or lugs on the columns. I have seen broken struts. A big beam settles, it puts a wrenching motion on the cast iron struts which support the beams. Naturally, they are not designed for standing such a strain. They are only for vertical loading. These broken struts or broken lugs on the columns were in my opinion due to settlement. I mean the heavy brick walls settled and these columns did not settle. There was quite a difference in level. There was a strain, and they had to break, being of cast iron. If they were steel, they might have bent. Plaintiff's Exhibit 70 illustrates what I mean. Those are portions of those brackets. Yes, here is another one put in there. In the background of this picture is a crack. The wall is only a tile partition. I saw the crack. The wall is a separation from the tunnel going down into the seats, only a partition wall. It does not support any beams or girders. In my opinion the crack in that wall was caused by the settlement of these beams. This wall rests on the beams. It went down and had to crack. The beam is the beam running toward the right hand side of the photograph as I hold it. As that settlement went down, it may have been as much as 15 or 16 inches between the column and the wall. That produced a wrenching motion and that had to crack. That part of the building needs to be watched as long as there is settlement, but if the settlement has stopped I do not look for any thing more of that kind. Those cracks were caused by settlement. I did not see any signs of plastering or recent repairs to any members when I was over there during the last two months. I think the last decorating in the theatre was four or five years ago.

Fireproofing was in its infancy at the time the Auditorium was built. Mr. White, Mr. Beitler and Mr. Eichler, three manufacturers of that class of material, were almost always in consultation with Mr. Adler on new ways of doing one thing or another. The floors all through the office and hotel building have tile arches. The steel members are protected by tile, excepting as I said before the columns under the sidewalk on that one floor on Congress Street. All the level portions of the theatre have tile arches but the sloped portions of the theatre; it was considered very difficult at the time. The method of putting wire lath and plaster underneath was considered fire protection from below. The space between the seats and the ceiling below was originally used for a chamber for the foul air to be taken away from the auditorium. There was no access to that space excepting for the engineer of the house, no public admittance or storage or anything of that kind was supposed to be in there. No fire could possibly get started in there. I am referring to the space which is shown in part of the photograph in evidence as Plaintiff's Exhibit 69. That is an elliptical ceiling over the auditorium, where the ventilation comes off. These are electric lights [indicating], thrown on the ceiling. That is all wire lath and plaster and channel bars. Above this a floor made of T-iron. Above that floor each member of the truss is individually fireproofed with tile. We would probably know better today how to do it than then. But the part below this floor and above the ceiling was considered protected from fire, and left unprotected with fireproofing.

That space is not used for anything at this time, except for the engineer to go in there and make alterations and replacements of electric lights or something connected with the ventilating system. These electric wirings could be put in metallic tubes as is done at the present time. I think it was done in advance of the engineering practices at that time. There wasn't any fireproofed theatre before the Auditorium. As far as the Auditorium was fireproofed, it was ahead of anything done in the City of Chicago.

I think all of the struts that were fractured or showed any signs of fracture have been taken care of. They have a very able man there who knows every nook and corner of that place.

I think we have seen the place shown in Plaintiff's Exhibition 59, on which Mr. Wade is pictured on the background. The flange at the bottom of the column could be fireproofed now. Half a pail of concrete would fix that. I don't know whether the column with wings on it, shown in Plaintiff's Exhibit 63, was part of the original design of the building or not. I went from bottom to top of that column to see whether there was the least sign of any deflection or any settlement. I could not find the smallest crack in any of the plaster on any of the ten stories. The only thing I can see as to why it was put in was to lower the floor there and for some mysterious reason they put the wings on. The floor has been lowered at the base under the column. There is a line through the other floor.

In Plaintiff's Exhibit 54 I see the straight edge across the floor. The floor lays on the ground. This happens to be the north wall, a heavy wall, which supports the banquet hall and so on. That settled and the floor went with it. It would be possible to dig a little deeper down and make the clearance greater. If that was done wherever the floor is high and the clearance low, the piping or sewer system, if they lay in the floor, would have to be lowered also. It can be changed as far as the height is concerned.

Mr. Adler was reputed at that time to be about as well posted on acoustics as anybody. He had built a number of theatres and churches previous to the Auditorium. He built the Central Music Hall on State and Randolph Street. That was a very fine theatre for acoustics. The Auditorium was achieved by not having any plaster inside the ceiling projecting on the solid walls. This was 35 years ago and we did not have the modern facilities for lathing and furring and so on. We made use of the primitive method of driving spikes in the wall and stretching wire, and then plastering on that. There were openings in the back of the theatre, on the stairs, and tunnels going into the theatre were left open to let the sound waves communicate with the floor above as well as the floor below. The result was that the Auditorium has been very successful as far as acoustics are concerned. You can hear in the last seat of the house almost as well as anywhere.

As to my experience in connection with caisson construction under existing buildings, and also in connection with the building of new buildings, I had the contract for the masonry on the first addition to Mandel Brothers' store. On State and Madison there was a pile foundation for the rest of the building, except that the north party wall had caissons. One of the caissons came under the accumulater for the elevators in the store, about 40 tons weight. That would travel up and down 25 or 30 feet with a pressure of 700 pounds to the square inch. Every once in a while when the elevators would go up that weight of 40 tons would come down with a bang under the foundation. I had to put a caisson directly under that, under the supervision of Mr. Thielbar and Mr. Fox. It took me six weeks. It was about as dangerous a piece of work as I ever undertook in my life, to keep that weight from pounding down where these men were down below digging for that caisson. But we got through with it without accident or without stopping the elevators in the Mandel Brothers' store for an hour. The next difficult thing I had to do was for the Brunswick-Balke-Collender Company. I built an addition to their factory. They had me enlarge the boiler room. One boiler came right in front of the chimney. The chimney is probably 120 or 130 feet high. The only way they could use the boiler was to make room for the shovelers and stokers to feed that boiler. I had to take the foundation out from under that chimney while it was in use, with burning boilers alongside it. I also had to guarantee not to disturb the factory. I took the foundation out and put columns there so as to make room for the stokers. The chimney had smoke coming out of it all the time we were working on it. Another complicated job was the tower of the Holy Name Cathedral; and I have had other experience besides those mentioned. As to my opinion whether caissons can be put under the Chicago Auditorium Building at this time if it becomes necessary to do so, well, of course, you can do so many things I don't see why the Auditorium could not be handled. It requires, of course, a good deal of careful attention. You cannot say right off. You have to go through it and examine it. If you could take the loads down in the basement, you may have to put it up to the second story and take the loads out there. No simple operation. I have not examined it closely enough to see whether there are any impossible arrangements there, but I imagine they can be overcome if there are any difficulties. Yes, there is some way physically by which the levels of these columns in the theatre could be made level with the exterior walls. Mr. Adler's scheme I think is feasible, and it would have been executed if he had been kept alive for a few months. When you enter the Auditorium foyer from the tower vestibule you go against the floor, which is the bow string. Naturally, the thousands of people who patronize the theatre continuously see the Auditorium has settled. Everybody knows it. Mr. Adler was very much interested that that should be changed. He wanted that floor level. He evolved an arrangment by which the columns would be sawed off on the bottom by using a horizontal steel saw and sawing off each column enough so that when lowered the floor would be level at that time with the settled Auditorium vestibule. He said to me, "Mueller, it seems that the Auditorium is getting to its home stretch." He meant the settlement was reduced, that he could undertake to lower that so that it would not have to be done over again. The sidewalks have been raised several times. He did not want to undertake the Auditorium until he thought the settlement had become about fixed on the main building. We would take off these pieces of the columns at the bottom in the basement. It would not be necessary, if we did that, to take out any of the columns on any of the higher floors. The auditorium is not connected with the rest of the building except as floor beams and girders go in. No heavy structural member is resting on those interior columns. By sawing this bottom off, of course you would have to hold up the whole weight of the auditorium building. On each column you would take as much off as it stood above the level of the vestibule, and then lower it. I do not regard that as a necessary step to take in order to maintain the present stability of the building, but just to make the floor level. That was Mr. Adler's idea, not to keep watching these struts that were replaced. I don't know whether they were all replaced under Mr. Adler's, but I know he continuously watched that feature of it. That operation could be performed without endangering the structural life of the building. It is dangerous if you handle it without doing it correctly. If well done, there should be no danger then. The Auditorium Building was a substantial and solid fireproof building of brick, stone, iron, tile and such other fireproofing materials as were necessary and usual in fireproofing buildings in the City of Chicago at the time it was erected. Yes, in fact, so much so that the building was continuously visited by the younger and older architects. I do not believe there is anybody in the profession that did not watch and look after the Auditorium while we were building it. The purpose of making the grillage foundation of different widths was that that had to be according to the load on each individual pier, had to be different according to the load. They are all sorts of sizes, no uniformity about it.

These people that went in and watched that Auditorium Building while it was being built, no, they were not apprehensive that the tower was going to go through to China. At the time when the building was being built no one knew there would be such a settlement as there was. The apprehension that the tower might go through to China arose when the load came on it, when the roof was on the building. I don't know whether there was a good deal of discussion after the roof was on and before the building was finished as to whether that tower was going to go through to China. There might have been talk about it, yet, I did not hear it. I did hear discussion about the sinking of the tower and settlement of the building while we were loading it with the bricks. I didn't hear of any architects and engineers going to look at this building on account of the settlement; not that I know of. I have read the "Autobiography of an Idea," written by Louis H. Sullivan, of Adler & Sullivan. . . .

Well, I think, Mr. Fisher, that at that time Mr. Sullivan speaks of what happened after the building was up and before. I think the Monadnock was built considerably after the Auditorium. I think it was 1890 that the Monadnock was built. The Auditorium, I think, was under roof in 1887. I think they were several years apart. Of course, the Auditorium tower settled the minute it was finished, we know that; but the way he applies it to the Monadnock block, that was after the building was up, and not before. The time they delayed about going on with the Monadnock building must have been before it was built, probably. I did say that people kept coming to the Auditorium, the architects and engineers, and visitors, and that they went in there to see it, a very remarkable structure. It might be they went in to see it in part to determine whether this floating foundation scheme of construction was going to work out; that might be, if it was known that it was going down. It was not known when the building was being built.

They put the organ in after the foundation and walls were up considerably. The walls went up to the top of the organ chamber, practically up to the ceiling of the auditorium. In the rear where this organ chamber was put, the wall was nearly up. The rest of the building was higher. I should say two-thirds of the way up. I think if the organ was put in at that time, that is some explanation of why the back wall keeps settling in the past five or six years, because the Studebaker or Fine Arts Building was added on top of that afterwards. I said I thought the place where this bench mark was was where they modified the construction of the rear of the Auditorium Building so as to put in the organ chamber. All those changes were made before 1890. I don't know exactly when the Studebaker addition was made. One of them, down below under the Studebaker Building, used as dressing rooms, I know that was made a number of years after the building was completed, three or four or five years, maybe. It has been there thirty odd years. If those loads were put on the Auditorium Building at that point thirty odd years ago, I don't know how that explains why the building is sinking at the place where the bench marks were made. That may have some different loading up there now. There may be some other reasons. I don't know of anything that has been added there in the past thirty years. I know they added the story on Michigan Avenue, which I didn't know about, too. As to why it is still going down there, one and a quarter inches within three or four years, it may be a section of that has not been compressed enough like it has been elsewhere. It might be the compression of different parts under this building has not gone far enough to stop the settling yet. I think the Auditorium and the Monadnock are both good examples of mason work. I think they represent the highest example of a type that has disappeared or is in the process of disappearing. . . .

They had a testing tank there for testing the ground in order to ascertain how much should be allowed for settlement. From that and other experience I was told to figure 2¼ tons per square foot of ground. As to how much that would settle, or how little, I had no knowledge. I don't know whether Mr. Adler made any computations as to how much or how little it would settle, but as far as I know, he gave the instructions for loading the ground 2¼ tons. There was no figure or computation made of which I have any knowledge by which it was undertaken to compute how much the building would settle. I heard Mr. Lichter testify that the instructions given to him were to allow for two inches in settlement. I have no information on that subject any more than that we allowed for additional settlement on account of the screws in the columns, which was six inches. The only thing I know in addition to the instructions given to Mr. Lichter to allow two inches was or is that there were four screws put in which would have given a play of six inches in the working of the screws. I did attach some significance in my direct testimony to the fact that the building has settled comparatively little in the last ten years. It may be possible that the levels produced in evidence in this case show that building settled in some points in the last ten years more than the full two inches allowed by Mr. Lichter in putting in the foundations originally. I have seen the table levels introduced in evidence here. I have a blue print in my pocket, and have had it there for several weeks. My testimony has been in part prepared on the basis of that blue print. I have no knowledge except from that. I see Pier No. 7 on the blue print. The level of that pier in April, 1915 was 13.75 feet. In 1924, nine years later, the level of that was 13.54. It sank two-tenths of a foot in those nine years, which would be something over 2 inches. Well, the 2 inches originally allowed for settlement was an upset above the grade. I don't know whether that could be called a complete settlement, because we had the screws for six inches. I have said Mr. Adler told me that the building might settle four or more inches. He meant that to be the total settlement in the building that would occur after it was constructed. At Pier 7 it started in 1887 at a level of 15.38 feet, and in 1912 it had got down to 13.74, a difference of about a foot and a half. In 1887 the level of Pier No. 7 was 15.38 feet, and its level in 1924, in the last column, was 13.54, a total settlement of 1.84 feet. It settled two-tenths in the last nine years.

In April, 1915 the level of Pier No. 16 was 13.52. In 1924 it was 13.22. It sank ⅒ of a foot, or one-half of the amount that pier No. 7 sank. In August, 1887, the level of Pier No. 16 and 15.45, and in 1924 it was 13.22. a total sinking in the whole period of the life of the building of 2.23 feet, or a little bit over 27 inches. Both piers settled with great irregularity, as compared with Pier No. 16, both during the entire life of the building and during the last ten years of the building. Pier No. 16 settled less than pier No. 7 in the last ten years. It settled just half. In the entire life of the building it settled 27 inches against about 22 inches. In other words, it settled in its entire life 5 inches more than the other pier did. That is more than the four inches. Mr. Adler said the whole thing might settle, and it is within one inch of the total capacity of these screws or jacks that were put in the columns. There weren't any jacks put in that had a bigger possibility of spread or difference of settlement of six inches. The difference in settlement between the two piers was almost the same as the total settlement allowed for in the jacks or screws.

I said there was some extra weight put on the tower, and that they tried to make it up by using some lighter material, tile. It was carefully figured out at the time to determine what additional load was put on the tower foundation to see how much more it would take and how much the hollow brick would reduce it. We carefully figured out how much the additional height and other additions would impose on the foundation. Then a computation was made, showing how much we could save in load by this change to tile. I can't recall now what the net result was, but it was almost balanced except for the mortar that would squeeze into the hollows of the hollow brick. That was an unknown quantity. It amounted to a substantial overload, I think. That overload, due to that mortar, is not in my opinion what caused that tower foundation to go down to the extent it did; it only caused the variation of the tower being lower than some other piers. It shows here that the tower settled about 8 inches more than the average of the other piers. It settled a good deal more than that average as between the tower and certain individual piers. I think that mortar that squeezed into those joints is what accounts for that 8 inches that the tower settled more than the average of the rest of the building. That was not only the mortar in the top of added stories; the hollow brick was used from down below, all the way up. We must have made a net saving in substituting hollow tile for the tile that had been figured. They were hollow. When we put the mortar in I shouldn't say that more than made up all the saving from substituting the hollow tile. The mortar didn't squeeze into the whole brick, only in the edges. The weight actually put on the tower foundation was figured for $2\frac{1}{4}$ tons. It was a little bit overloaded. They actually put on a little more than $2\frac{1}{4}$ tons. I couldn't say exactly how much. I doubt if it run it up to 3 tons. I would simply have to guess at it. I haven't got those figures anymore. I could not guess whether it increased it another half ton or not. The weight of $2\frac{1}{4}$ tons in pounds would be 4500 pounds. The load allowed under the present building ordinance is 3500. My judgment is that the load actually put on the tower foundation was more than 4500 pounds per square foot, due to the mortar, and the present load that would be allowed on a foundation of that character, under the building ordinance, is 3500 pounds. The tower foundation of the Auditorium is not overloaded 50 per cent, as compared with the present allowance under the building code; it would be the difference between 35 and 45. I couldn't say just exactly what it is. It is something substantial. There was a substantial addition to the 4500 pounds per square foot actually put on that foundation, due to this mortar. I couldn't say whether it was increased 500 pounds; it might be. I haven't got those figures. It might have been 500 pounds. That would mean that the total weight would be 5,000 pounds per square foot. I said it was a substantial addition to the 4,500 that was made, and that it might have been 500. I say it might have been, but I can't say that it was. It was more than 100 pounds, between 200 and 500 I should say. That would make the load on the tower foundation 4700 pounds per square foot, and the load allowed by the present building ordinance is 3500 pounds. They allow more than 3500 on hard clay, but I assume this structure is on soft clay. It would be somewhere from 4700 to 5000 which taking the minimum, is an overload of 1200 pounds per square foot, as compared with the present ordinance, or something like 34 per cent. If it was 500 pounds, there would be an overload of 1500 pounds, or about 40 per cent. I have said that the result of this operation would, in my opinion, have been the sinking of the tower to such an extent it would have broken away from the rest of the building if it had not been for the fact we put some steel beams down in the bottom of that foundation; I don't know that I can say that is the only thing that saved it. The walls might have spread it over without the beams. When the additional weight was put in other parts of the building, like the banquet hall, and the organ loft, there was not anything done to strengthen the foundations carrying those loads. I can't say how much overload added, but it was considerable. There was no addition made to take care of that extra load. I never had anything personally to do myself with any building in the City of Chicago that sank 28 inches after it was built. I had buildings 8 inches. That is about the most I had. That is anywhere in the world. I think the most in the City of Chicago is four inches.

I testified that these foundations had to go down so low below the grade because it was necessary to get a timber grillage below the general water level. It would have been better, from the point of view of structural stability, for the foundations to have been only down where they would rest on the blue clay, if we had found any, but I don't recollect there was any hard pan or clay found on the Auditorium site. If there had been any of this blue clay or upper hard pan, it would have been better if the foundations had rested on it. Yes, if the hard clay had been there. Ordinarily in Chicago you go down 10 to 15 feet from grade and then come to a level of blue clay or hard pan, but down there in that locality, I don't think you will find that hard clay.

I saw the foundations of the Monadnock go in. My recollection is they probably did not go more than 13 or 14 feet, and they rested on the blue clay or hard pan, on the upper crust. That is the principle reason why this method of using steel beams, I-beams, for a grillage, was adopted in this city; it followed the Auditorium building in time. When the Auditorium building was built that method was not used. They didn't use timber. The only other timber foundation I know of in the City of Chicago is the Board of Trade Building. They discontinued putting in grillage on hard pan, blue clay, or any other kind of thing, in foundatons of the large buildings in the City of Chicago immediately after the completion of the Chicago Auditorium building. They used piles and afterwards caissons for higher buildings. They discontinued that method for higher buildings.

The statement with respect to the Monadnock Building, that it was the first and last word of its kind; a gread word in its day; but its day vanished almost overnight, leaving it to stand as a symbol, as a solitary monument, marking the high tide of masonry construction as applied to commercial structures,—well, that is Mr. Sullivan's language, and, of course, that is the language of literature and romance. Substantially, I think it is correct. . . .

And in connection with this, I might say that some engineers were employed on the Auditorium. There was Mr. Strobel and there was Mr. Marburg, the Keystone Bridge Company. They handled the trusses. These men belong to the class of gentlemen who subsequently saw this vision of steel structure, and they have helped solve it. When the Auditorium was built, of course, we had masonry walls. We have a skeleton wall in the court of the hotel. The south wall of the court in the hotel is the skeleton wall. I would not compare that with what is called the modern steel construction, but it is a stepping stone to it. And we had some steel beams down under the tower, and used a few steel beams in the building. My recollection is the Auditorium was one of the first buildings that got the steel from the Homestead Mills that was changed over, so that it is now making Bessemer steel. Formerly it had been making wrought iron. As to what the beams it furnished to the Auditorium building were in fact, I do know that at one time a channel fell down on the floor or the ground, instead of going down on the skids, as it usually did, and that channel cracked. That would not have happened if it was wrought iron, so that particular channel must have been of steel. Whether the beams generally used were steel can easily be ascertained. You couldn't turn a whole plant over into the making of steel and make wrought iron at the same time. It meant a complete revolution. We had to go down there. Mr. Adler had to go down there. We had a man down there to report on the continuance of the steel. I did not hear Mr. Renwick testify. If Mr. Renwick, having been there and watched it, said in his deposition that the beams in the Auditorium were wrought iron, that would not have anything to do with my opinion. I went to Mr. Strobel's office to find out and heard from his partner that the mill was changed in 1883, and after that all of the other mills followed suit. I do know Mr. Adler went down to Pittsburgh, we had other men to report on the processs of rolling these beams, so as to get them into the building, and I do know the building was put up in a lopsided way, waiting for these beams. I went to Mr. Strobel's office and tried to find out, and could not find out what was actually furnished to the Auditorium. Mr. Strobel was not there. I found out from his partner that the Homestead mill had been changed to the manufacture of Bessemer steel. That was all I found out.

The load per square foot for the banquet hall was figured at 75 pounds. The present ordinance allows 100 pounds to the square foot as the bearing capacity of the beams and columns. Some other cities require only 75 pounds. I don't think I know any of less.

Acoustics have been a matter of accident. For instance, the very noted acoustics in the Salt Lake City Tabernacle was an accident. When they put in the gallery, if that gallery had gone tight to the wall, that acoustic would have been spoiled, but it just happened by accident they kept away so as not to hit their head on the curved dome, and the acoustics remained the same as it was before. Nearly every theatre or hall that has such a cut off space shows very poor acoustics.

All the columns in the Auditorium are of cast iron. I don't think there are any steel columns. In the office and hotel the iron and steel columns and girders are fireproofed, except where the floors are level. The sloping portion of the theatre has beams only protected from underneath with lath and plaster. The steel columns and girders that are fireproofed are covered with porous terra cotta and plaster, excepting the small columns under the sidewalk and under the first floor. I don't think any of the beams or girders are covered with concrete directly on the beam or girder. I doubt it, because it was previous to the days we used concrete fireproofing. We use it now. It is regarded as the better method when we have a concrete floor. Just lately in the Morrison Hotel they are using tile again. The use of concrete in the art of fireproofing was practically started at the Union Trust Building in St. Louis, which was built by Mr. Probst of the Probst Construction Company, of which Mr. Lichter and myself are members, and there with the fireproofing around the floor beams striking into the columns on the outside, it was always difficult to get the terra cotta to fit, and that was fireproofed with concrete. The fireproofing companies have generally taken advantage of that, and since then have almost invariably used concrete made of the remnants of broken tile, and the columns are quite frequently now fireproofed in that method. I should say that is advance in the art of fireproofing.

I should say that all of the beams, joists and roofing beams and joints are iron and steel. All of the constructional floors are arches of hollow tile or like materials excepting the balconies to the theatre. Those are just wood. All the partitions are of brick or hollow tile, as far as I know. There may be some temporary wooden partitions. The roof is of iron, brick or hollow tile. It is fireproof construction. There are steel beams up there, too. Generally speaking, steel would be included under the general term iron. Where they use steel instead of what is strictly called iron, I would regard that as a compliance with the terms of the lease from which you are reading. . . .

You use the word "iron"—steel belongs to the original word "iron." It is evolved from iron. There are companies that manufacture steel that still call themselves iron companies. This fireproofing of the columns and other foundations I have mentioned was done according to the best known building practices of the time at which the building was put up. There were no jackscrews put under any of the piers that I know of. There were jackscrews on the north wall, on the adjoining building, under the continuous wall, the party wall for the adjoining building. When I testified about pier 7 and pier 16, I did not mean to let the impression be that there were any jackscrews under those piers. The jackscrews under the columns under the sidewalk and those supporting one floor along on the Congress street side are all I know of. . . .

That channel that fell on the ground and broke is the only one I recall, because I happened to see it, and Mr. Adler remarked, "That is the way all steel is sold us to be so much strength, but give me wrought iron. That would not break like that." They had a man in Pittsburgh to look after the tests applied to those beams. He was supposed to test the material before it was rolled. I never new any other case where a channel of steel broke under such circumstances.

From Bruce Pfeiffer, Taliesin West, April 11, 1988

Dear Edgar,

I believe that in the autobiography Mr. Wright describes Mueller and his role with Sullivan, and also his role in the Imperial Hotel construction.

The only personal "recollection" I seem to dredge out of my memory is Mrs. Wright's description of Paul Mueller staying with them at Ocotilla working on the engineering drawings for the San Marcos project. She described him as a kind and wonderful gentleman; whenever he came back from the town of Chandler he always brought some little gifts for Iovanna and Svet, a bracelet of silver and turquoise (inexpensive in those days), a beaded bag, something charming. He was a powerfully-built man, Mrs. Wright said, German, with an imposing beard. He had great force of direction and supervision, was never nervous or troubled, could tackle any problem and cope with all human (as well as inhuman) problems. But he was also obedient to cause. He told Mrs. Wright that when he was building the Imperial Hotel, one day while he was at home his wife was making fudge. The chocolate was on the stove cooking, but when adding the sugar she realized that she was about to run out of it. "Paul, I must rush down to the market for more sugar. Take the pot off the stove, and keep stirring it so that it will not stiffen until I get back with the sugar!" He went on to explain to Mrs. Wright "I took that pot, placed it on the kitchen table, and continued to stir as instructed. Suddenly there was a minor earthquake — everything began to slide and move around the room; the kitchen chairs moved, the table I was sitting at moved, I moved, but I kept right on stirring that fudge! Because regardless of what damage the tremblor might do to the house, it could not match the wrath of Mrs. Mueller if I had deserted my post and neglected her fudge!"

I think that tells a great deal about him, or about Mrs. Mueller however you wish to read it. But Mrs. Wright had only fine admiration for him, as did Mr. Wright. And of course the little girls were thrilled to see him come across the desert with his usual delights for them tucked into his pockets . . .

That is about all I can do [to] help.

We still have all his data-sheets from the preliminary studies of the hotel and its tests for the pile-foundations.

Frank Lloyd Wright and 'The Sovereignty of the Individual'

One of the monuments of Frank Lloyd Wright's career is the double portfolio, *Ausgeführte Bauten und Entwürfe,* issued by Wasmuth in Berlin in 1910. One hundred plates printed in gentle tints show drawings, all of which Wright carefully revised for this edition. They were accompanied by his untitled introductory essay translated into German. Forty years later Wright decided to reuse this essay in the catalogue of a grand exhibition of his architecture circulated throughout Europe; later, versions of it were seen in Mexico and the United States. He now entitled the essay "The Sovereignty of the Individual," a phrase only tenuously related to the text. Why did Wright use this phrase, what did it mean to him? Answers may lie in Wright's circumstances as he originally organized the portfolios in the hills above Florence in the winter of 1909–1910.

Wright's agreement with Wasmuth had been reached in 1909 when he first visited Europe. He was accompanied by Mamah Bouton Borthwick Cheney, the wife of a client; the ensuing scandal has become an often-repeated element of the Wright legend. Mamah divorced in 1911, but for years Catherine Wright refused to liberate her

husband. Despite many separations Mamah remained Wright's companion and close associate until her dreadful murder (at Taliesin, the country home Wright had built for them both) in 1914 while he was in Chicago.

From the start of their relationship Wright responded to Mamah's intellectual interests. The two appeared as joint translators of *Love and Ethics* by Ellen Key, the Swedish feminist, issued in Chicago by Ralph Fletcher Seymour in 1912. A year earlier Seymour had published another book by Ellen Key, translated by Mrs. Cheney. Two more such tracts appeared in 1912; one, *The Woman Movement,* introduced by Havelock Ellis, was published in New York by G.P. Putnam's Sons (reprinted in 1976 by Hyperion Press, Westport, Connecticut).

Both Seymour and Wright had offices in the Fine Arts Building in Chicago, and in that building in 1914, Margaret Anderson initiated her famous *Little Review.* Wright praised it freely. In her editorials Miss Anderson used the phrase, "the sovereignty of the individual," and lauded Ellen Key. A year after the tragedy at Taliesin the *Little Review* published a translation of a "Hymn to Nature," ascribed to Goethe while the translators were called only "a strong man and a strong woman." (Goethe, toward the end of his life, had hesitantly acknowledged this fragmentary manuscript dated 1783.) Again in 1915 Miss Anderson printed Mamah Borthwick's translation of Ellen Key's tribute to Romain Rolland, reviled as a pacifist but just crowned with a Nobel Prize for Literature. These events suggest that Frank Lloyd Wright continued to foster Mamah Borthwick's ideas and work even after her death.

Why were Wright and Mamah kindred spirits as well as lovers? Mamah Borthwick had left home to work as a teacher and librarian, and for five years, it has been said, she rejected the marriage proposal of a former schoolmate, Edwin Cheney, whom she finally accepted. Although she bore him two children she often left them in the care of her sister or others, and seemed more interested in intellectual pursuits. In short, she was an individualist more than a wife and mother. Wright had grown up in a tense household, often on the move, with a feckless father, a man of charm and education but without the ability to support his wife, their children, or his children by a deceased earlier wife. Even the help of his new wife's imposing brother, Jenkin Lloyd Jones, did not avail. Finally, Anna Wright (who seems to have suffered acutely from a disorder of the genital tract and could not serve her husband's sexual wants) insisted that the household move to Madison, Wisconsin, where her brothers could contribute from their farms to the needs of everyday life.[1] And, in return, her eleven-year-old son could be trained to help on the farm throughout the summer when all hands were welcome. This left him some months each winter to aug-

ment his schooling. In short, he was cast in the role of a juvenile breadwinner, whose friends and mentors were individualists, not a cohesive family. At eighteen young Wright sensibly ran away to Chicago, where he could be more free and earn money to share with his mother, recently divorced, and his sisters. It did not take long for the women to join him in Chicago. Yet he was by now an independent individual, and soon enough he married. But young Frank Lloyd Wright's household, with eventually six children, never seemed to him, nor to his sons who recalled their childhood, a cohesive family. Companionship and affection were available, but the unity of a home was lacking. The dining room with its high-backed chairs enclosing assorted eaters enhanced a social ritual, but nothing more. Thus it is possible to see how both Mamah and Wright were accustomed to consider themselves free individuals, free to form their lives as they believed was right.

When one considers Mamah's affiliation with the women's movement, and the fact that an elevated concept of free love was the basis of the association between her and Wright, it seems possible that she was the one to draw his attention to the phrase, "the sovereignty of the individual." Her interests and training might have led her to a book of 1889, published in Boston by Benjamin R. Tucker, an early convert to the idea of free love. This was Stephen Pearl Andrews's, *Love, Marriage, and Divorce and the Sovereignty of the Individual. A Discussion with Henry James [Senior], Horace Greeley, and Stephen Pearl Andrews, rejected by the Tribune, and a consequent discussion, occurring twenty years later, between Mr. James and Mr. Andrews.* (Greeley was the founding editor of the *New York Trib-*

une.) A judicious excerpt can be read in Taylor Stoehr, *Free Love in America*, New York, AMS Press, 1979. Long before, Andrews had explained the concept in September 1857, in "The Sovereignty of the Individual" in *The Periodical Letter* edited by Josiah Warren. Andrews wrote, "the logical and legitimate termination of the Democratic idea is in the Sovereignty of every Individual within the limit that it is not to be exercised at the cost of others. . . . The individual has an absolute right to his own time, to a companionship of his own choice, to his own habits and characteristics, to the privilege even of whimsical inconsistency, provided it be not of a kind to invade the Sovereignty of others." Andrews was also a believer in free love, unlike his mentor, Warren, who had expressed his ideas less eloquently in the November 1854 issue of *The Periodical Letter:* "Societary institutions should be made for man, and not man for institutions. . . . All laws for the guidance of men in their social or collective state should be in strict accordance with the natural law of individuality, or they are unjust, and must prove subversive." (Quoted from Stoehr.) It is worthwhile to compare these American statements with those of John Stuart Mill. He was writing "On Liberty" in collaboration with his beloved wife in that same year, 1854, though the essay was not published until 1859. He says: "Over himself, over his own mind, the individual is sovereign. . . . It is only individuality which produces, or can produce, well developed human beings." In these statements one can hear echoes of Emerson's "Self-Reliance" (whose first series of *Essays* was published in 1841 and soon thereafter in England).

Now it seems possible to estimate how central to Wright's whole way of thinking was this phrase, 'the sovereignty of the individual.' It was not merely a justification of his own unconventional actions, it was intimately linked to his concepts of ceaseless change, of emergent democracy, of creativity in the arts. One manifestation of change — technology — weakened small societies able to impose local mores; each individual now needed to discover within, the principles by which to live. On the strength and depth of such efforts depended the validity of a democratic society; anything less was bound to lead to exploitation and tyranny. The prevailing marriage laws were examples of this; and so was the spiritless copying which Wright saw permeating the work of the Prairie School architects. Such confined ingrowth seemed to him to obstruct life in harmony with the great principles of nature, guiding prolific change. That is why his rejections of his first marriage and his successful career were not only simultaneous but essentially identical. To be free to grow, Wright believed, was the only way to honor life.

In later years Wright insisted on using the word *individuality.* Similarly, he trained apprentices by dint of repeated contradictions, no rules were sacred. What Wright sought to teach was self-discovery and self-reliance, not recipes which could save a follower the trouble of being an individual. Wright knew well, what is evident today, that the era of styles was over, even a modern style. He relied on Buffon's "style is the man himself." He had no desire to serve as a model for imitators, he hoped for architects who would discover and strengthen the unique potentials of their clients and of the environments in which they lived. It was sovereignty of, by, and for the individual in which he had faith as the instrument of accomplishment in a universe of change.

NOTE

1 Anna Wright's physical troubles are indicated by two quotations to be found in Brendan Gill, *Many Masks,* New York, 1987. First, he says, William Wright stated during divorce proceedings: "About three years ago . . . she refused to occupy the same bed with me . . . and for two years last past she has not occupied the same room with me at night." Ref. pp. 52, 53. Then, he says, Anna's stepdaughter, Elizabeth (who in her seventies wrote an account of her life, an unpublished manuscript kept by the Iowa State Historical Society, Iowa City), wrote about Anna, "She seemed to have periodic spells when she got 'mad hysterics' and raved like a maniac. Then she would be sick in bed for a day or two . . . " Ref. p. 42.

Precedent and Progress in the Work of Frank Lloyd Wright

"Progress before Precedent"—that unthinking, unthinkable thing! Frank Lloyd Wright said in 1914.[1] He was well aware of the role of precedent in his architectural development, and wrote about it on several occasions. One precedent which gave rise to a central characteristic of his mature work he did not mention, however—an unlikely precedent for Wright—the inglenook. What is it? A hearth (ingle) in its own alcove (nook) usually including seats. How did Wright encounter it, did it attract other designers of the day, what became of it at his hands?

Looking backward, the inglenook can be identified clearly by the late fifteenth century.[2] In Tudor England then the yeomen were rising in prominence and evolved a distinctive form of substantial farmhouse with marked features, the inglenook being one. Beginning with seating of some kind arranged within the ample chimney breast of a working kitchen, sheltering one or two people from the prevalent cold, it was changed to a more seemly form, rather like

Reprinted from the *Journal of the Society of Architectural Historians,* May 1980.

a window embrasure, ensconced in the fireplace of the hall. FIGS. 22, 23. It became a snug alcove off a main room, suggesting companionable intimacy. I've not found in the literature how common or uncommon inglenooks may have been in the sixteenth century in Britain. For a while, anyway, they held their place until classicism showed them the door.

Inglenooks were revived in the mid-1860s by two clever and enthusiastic young architects, Eden Nesfield and Norman Shaw.[3] FIGS. 24, 25. From them the fashion spread rapidly throughout British drafting rooms and within a decade it was adopted by advanced designers in America. On both sides of the Atlantic, despite increasing use of central heating, architects liked the coziness of inglenooks and the dramatic shift of scale from large room to tight alcove. At first dwarf windows were incorporated at either side of the fireplace admitting localized light for reading and needlework. The featured area was more richly detailed and decorated than the room around it, often a dining room which thus could double as an extra sitting area.

American architects, led by H.H. Richardson, designed inglenooks based chiefly on those

FIG. 22. Inglenook in cooking area, Abbas Hall near Sudbury, Suffolk, remodeled, mid-fifteenth century. Seat at left with adjacent recess for cup.

FIG. 24. W. Eden Nesfield, Farnham Park, Bucks., 1865, inglenook.

FIG. 23. Inglenook added to hall, Speke Hall, Liverpool, in early sixteenth century.

FIG. 25. R. Norman Shaw, Willesley, Cranbrook, Kent, 1864–65, inglenook in dining room.

FIG. 26. H.H. Holly, *Modern Dwellings in Town and Country*, 1878, grand staircase.

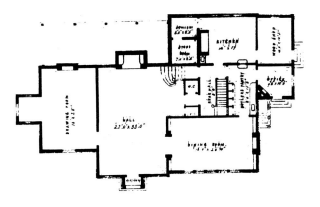

FIG. 28. H.H. Richardson, Codman house project, 1869–71, inglenook in hall.

FIG. 27. R. Norman Shaw, own house, London, 1876, dining room inglenook, private drafting room above.

of Shaw, whose works were well published. FIGS. 27, 28. However, the Americans accented associational values differently than the Victorians: overt hospitality was emphasized more than quiet intimacy. Moreover, once Shaw had shown the way in his own town house, the country-bred character of inglenooks was overlooked and they were accepted in city and suburban homes, as a matter of fact more freely in America than in Britain. FIG. 26.

In time changes were rung on the theme. Particularly, one begins to find inglenooks, hearths included, underneath main staircases, with upper galleries looking down into the hall. This location made the inglenook a pivot for the movements of sociability and family life; now more than a quaint feature, it tended to symbolize the idea of home. FIG. 29. Other variations were tried by well-known architects.[4] FIGS. 30, 31, 33, 34.

It was Richardson, however, more than anyone who set the tone for American architecture

70

FIG. 29. John Calvin Stevens, interior of Thaxter Cottage, ca. 1885.

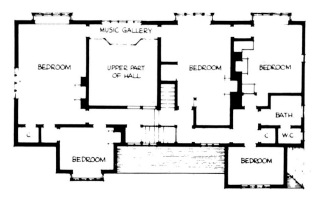

FIG. 31. M.H. Baillie Scott, Bexton Croft, Knutsford, Cheshire, 1895, upper floor plan, inglenook in bedroom at right.

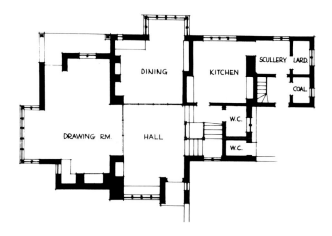

FIG. 30. Ernest George, cottage, Harpenden, Herts., ca. 1888, inglenook in drawing room.

FIG. 32. Frank Lloyd Wright, own house, Oak Park, Illinois, as remodeled 1895. Compare to original plan of 1889, FIG. 12 in H.-R.Hitchcock's *In the Nature of Materials.*

in the 1880s; his art predominated more than Shaw's overseas. Young Wright, hardly in his twenties, inevitably began to design architecture in fairly Richardsonian forms, influenced by the two men he worked for in turn, J.L. Silsbee and Louis H. Sullivan. The inglenook entered his repertory at the very start of his career. In 1886 or early 1887, before leaving

FIG. 33. Adolf Loos, hall project, ca. 1901? Some scholars date this to the 1890s.

FIG. 34. J.M. Olbrich, own house, Darmstadt, 1901, hall. Olbrich and Baillie Scott shared the patronage of the Grand Duke of Hesse.

Madison, Wisconsin, for Chicago, Wright designed a little chapel project in the Silsbee manner where an inglenook lends an unusually domestic air to a rural community structure. This does not seem inept, in plan at least, and already indicates Wright's individuality. I've not found an inglenook in the residential designs Wright carried out for Sullivan in the years 1888 to 1893.

It was 1889 when Wright built his own small home and opened a new chapter in the history of inglenooks. FIG. 32. Paying slight heed to historic references, Wright combined current details into a unit of notable originality. An inglenook, three by eight and a half feet, occupied the heart of the house opening to the living room to reveal a low, round-arched fireplace of brick and on each side a stiff wooden bench; above one bench an opening connected inglenook and dining room. Continuous friezes made the rooms appear higher than the nook. Benches and masonry fireplace, as well as the seeming change of height, conformed to British precedent, but the dominant position and openings connecting main rooms gave this inglenook new meaning. This inglenook is not only a symbol of domesticity, it is the physical core of the structure and from it elements of the house jut outward to make contact with the exterior environment.

In 1889 one might have thought this inglenook a superfluous elaboration in a closely budgeted home; today it can be recognized as the seed from which was to spring one of Wright's main architectural means. By 1904 or 1905, when he had matured his Prairie School manner of design, virtually all of Wright's houses were extended from cores identified with chimneys and fireplaces, while his buildings for business and worship, namely, the Larkin Building and Unity Temple, were similarly centered around cores—of space, not matter. His first

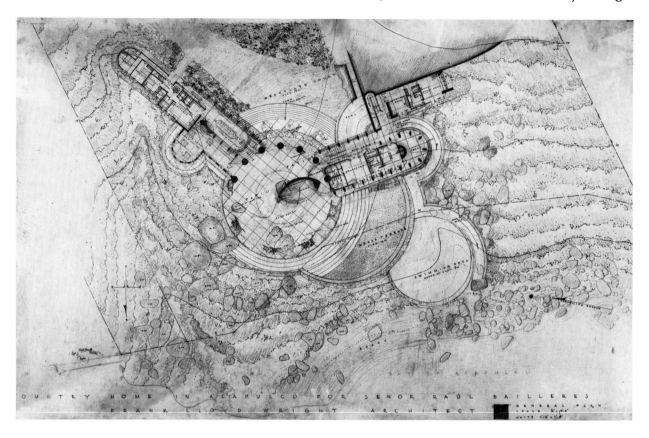

FIG. 35.   Frank Lloyd Wright, Bailleres house project, Acapulco, 1952, nook at center.

independent structure, his home in Oak Park, managed to demonstrate both possibilities: its inglenook combines a core of space and a core of matter. Wright's great works in the first decade of this century, the rich outpouring that established him as an architect of high genius, remain tantalizing until the seminal role of the inglenook is realized.

The shift from treating inglenooks as picturesque addenda to treating them as symbols of home was occurring almost simultaneously in Britain and the United States. Now Wright intuitively was pushing ahead of this, approaching the insight that was to guide his designing for the next half-century: the realization that the essence of architectural expression was control of space, and that mastery over materials and technologies was ancillary to the mastery of space, that is, the ability to characterize spatially the nuances and relationships of human needs and aspirations. Not surprisingly, the inglenook suffered many alterations in the course of this

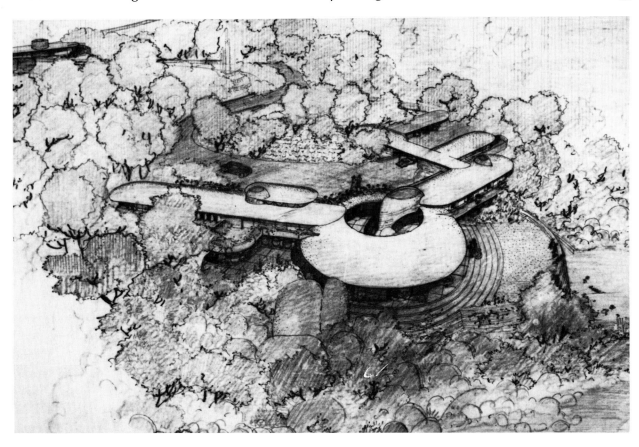

FIG. 36. Frank Lloyd Wright, Bailleres house project, aerial view. The nook, visible through skylight, contains a fountain and "air-conditioner."

evolution. Its mutations proceeded from the enclosed core, to the half-open core, to the liberated core — an island that coordinates spaces around it; yet the core always included a hearth and some trace of an alcove. Wright was not the only explorer in this architectural area, but he was the most active. The fascination of Wright's architecture lies in great part in the unhurried consistency and profound ingenuity with which he pursued these possibilities. It is worthwhile to look at a late example of his work in this light.[5] FIGS. 35, 36.

This random survey of inglenooks and their sequels allows a few conclusions to be drawn. What begins as a somewhat bookish reevocation of an ancient, prosaic device soon assumes greater importance: it becomes a symbol of social ideals. Transported across an ocean, this development loses some associations while gaining related ones of lesser subtlety. At the hands of a young American designer the theme, already liberally interpreted by many architects, evolves into new, terse, and eloquent arrangements. This shift removes it from the historic and societal associations long established, giving it fresh power in which human meaning, aesthetic deftness, and architectural cogency combine to form an important and original advance. Precedent prepared the way for progress even though precedent alone never could have led to so much radical innovation.

NOTES

This paper was originally prepared for a talk to the students of architecture at the University of Manchester, England, an occasion instigated by Professor Trevor Dannatt, H.F.A.I.A.

Architectural examples cited but not illustrated here are easily found in Henry-Russell Hitchcock, *In the Nature of Materials: 1887–1941; the Buildings of Frank Lloyd Wright*, New York, 1942; H.-R. Hitchcock, *The Architecture of H.H. Richardson and His Times*, Hamden, Conn., rev. ed., 1961; and Andrew Saint, *Richard Norman Shaw* (Studies in British Art), New Haven, 1976. A nucleus of historical information was provided by Mark Girouard, *The Victorian Country House*, Oxford, 1971, and *Country Life*, 30 August and 6 September 1973. Further examples of inglenooks can be seen in Hermann Muthesius, *Das moderne Landhaus und seine innere Ausstattung*, Munich, 2nd rev. and enl. ed., 1905; James D. Kornwolf, *M.H. Baillie Scott and the Arts and Crafts Movement; Pioneers of Modern Design*, Baltimore, 1972; Vincent J. Scully, *The Shingle Style and the Stick Style; Architectural Theory and Design from Richardson to the Origins of Wright*, New Haven, rev. ed., 1971; and H. Allen Brooks, *The Prairie School; Frank Lloyd Wright and His Mid-West Contemporaries*, Toronto, 1972. Joseph

T. Butler and David G. De Long kindly advised on early American inglenooks. Avery Memorial Library provided rich resources and courteous help. Robert L. Sweeney, *Frank Lloyd Wright: An Annotated Bibliography*, Los Angeles, 1978, proved to be valuable.

1 This slogan of the Architectural League of America had been criticized by Wright as early as 1900. See Sweeney, *Frank Lloyd Wright*, nos. 38 and 124.

2 An outdoor museum at Cardiff is said to show relocated houses with inglenooks. The phrase, *sous le manteau de la cheminée*, suggests that inglenooks played a role in polite usage across the Channel. Simple examples (some encompass bedsteads) survive in north-European peasant homes, but they are difficult to date. In Colonial times in North America inglenooks were arranged in one-room houses or kitchens. Seemingly this modest usage had no effect on American architecture of the later nineteenth century.

3 Apparently inglenooks were revived far earlier in nonresidential buildings. The two grand rooms at the northwest corner of the Reform Club by Charles Barry, London, 1838–1840, one on each main floor, have inglenooks, one Ionic and the other Corinthian in detail. Perhaps research would reveal more early examples. I remain indebted to the late Hon. Godfrey Samuel for the opportunity to visit the Reform Club.

4 H. Muthesius, in the third volume of *Das englische Haus, Entwicklung, Bedingungen, Anlage, Aufbau, Einrichtung und Innenraum*, 3 vols., Berlin, 1905, illustrates a ready-made inglenook!

5 See, e.g., Wright's Winslow house, Taliesin, and Wingspread in Hitchcock, *In the Nature of Materials*.

'The New Order of This Machine Age'

Frank Lloyd Wright, composing his autobiography in the late 1920s, used this phrase to characterize the creation of the famous (but now destroyed) Larkin Building in Buffalo in 1904. His words take on clearer meaning when one considers the development of one small element of the building, a semicircular reception desk in the lobby. This desk has eluded discussion even in Jack Quinan's excellent book on the building;[1] nevertheless, without his investigations this study could not have been pursued.

Quinan vividly describes the approach to the building's main entrance: a smooth sheet of water fell to one side of a pathway which stepped up until it was possible to appreciate the explicatory bas-relief from which the water issued and a long rectangular pool into which it descended. Ahead, in a recess, were very large clear glass doors and a huge transom, all echoed at the far end of the lobby. Once inside, on the left lay the prominent desk and on the right a flat, monumentally long fireplace; its partly carved ashlar mantel framed an opening opposite the desk. Overhanging the fireplace was a shallow balcony where visitors might write home (it was hoped, in praise of the Larkin enterprise).

A preliminary glance at two photographs published by Quinan (FIGS. 37, 38) will help to explain eight early sketches for the reception desk. These, presented on one sheet, are entirely in Wright's own hand (FIG. 39), unlike many drawings supervised by him. This sheet was released by the Frank Lloyd Wright Memorial Foundation in their first sale of redundant holdings. It shows three slightly different floor plans of the desk followed by variant elevations or, in one instance, a perspective view.

Later in life Wright was to advocate conceiving a whole building with all its chief details before putting pencil to paper; however, this skill required some years of experience. Wright wrote in his autobiography how essential changes occurred to him before the final drawings for the Larkin Building. Jack Quinan adduces more refinements of this intricately organized mail-order office building. It is not then surprising to find the architect sketching alternative versions of the reception desk, which guided the flow of people in the lobby.

The desk served people with inquiries; backed up to it and opening to the main office spaces were two elevators for the essential mail, incoming and outgoing, and for passengers, at

The lobby of the Larkin Administration Building is in full harmony with the spirit of the Larkin institution.

FIG. 37.   Frank Lloyd Wright, Larkin Building, Buffalo, New York, 1904. Reception desk in lobby.

set times going to or leaving the top-floor restaurant. Inserted between desk and elevators were telephone switchboards handling numerous interoffice as well as exterior calls. The operators were shielded in part from the noise and movement of a busy headquarters building. Thus the desk was but the prow of a group of

diverse elements, positioned with regard to two massive structural piers and kept well below the high ceiling of the main floor.

Frank Lloyd Wright's sheet of autograph drawings shows how he approached the forming of the reception desk. It seems reasonable to read the drawings as if they were so many col-

FIG. 38.   Frank Lloyd Wright, Larkin Building reception desk, a later view.

umns of text. The first of these (to the left) shows a plan where a rather slim, curved desk is bracketed by rectangular blocks not aligned with the great structural piers behind them. FIG. 40. The link of desk to block seems clear, yet some variations are indicated to the left. The block to the right is elaborated with partly cir- cular detail. Behind the desk four seats are shown at a bank of switchboards. Set well be- hind these is a barrier against two elevators. At one end of the switchboards a group of four lamps has been roughed in; such lamps occur also in twos and singly throughout the building. Each lamp consisted of two milk glass hemi-

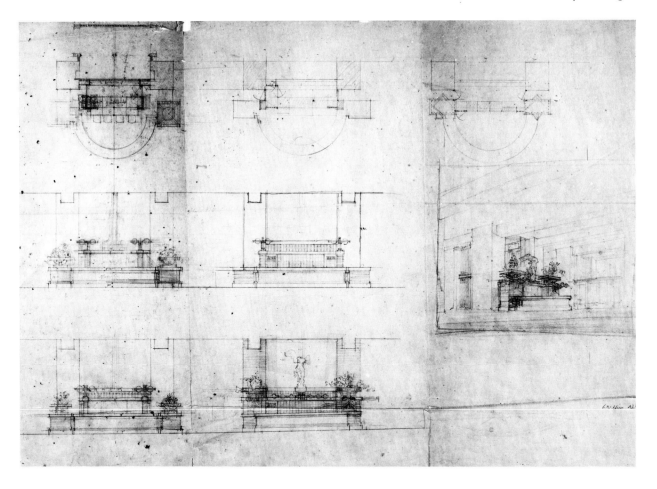

FIG. 39.   Frank Lloyd Wright, developmental studies for reception desk in Larkin Building, ca. 1903.

spheres, joined by a metal frame to form a globe.[2] The sketch plan also shows that entrances to the desk area and passages within it were narrow.

Below the first plan is an elevation which makes Wright's scheme more understandable. The blocks to each side are of brick and kept even with the desktop. Each block bears a low bowl with bold rim and base, and with small wedging blocks (a detail used variously throughout the building). The bowls are filled with plants. Behind, one sees panels of switchboards, framed by brick piers, very slender ones, which hold the light fixtures just mentioned. Above this panel a central plinth is lightly penciled, bearing a filmy indication of a

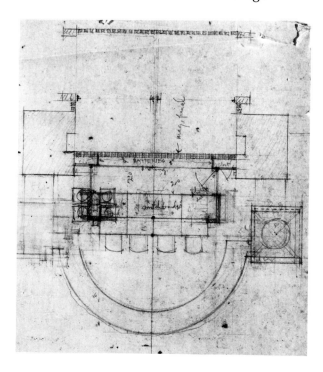

FIG. 40. Frank Lloyd Wright, first plan from studies in FIG. 39.

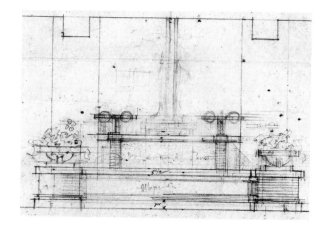

FIG. 41. Frank Lloyd Wright, first elevation from plan in FIG. 40.

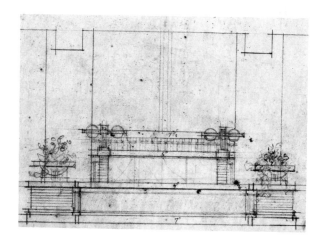

FIG. 42. Frank Lloyd Wright, second elevation from plan in FIG. 40.

large figure, possibly winged, whose immediate purpose is to mask the vertical rails of the twin elevators. FIG. 41. Finally, Wright was concerned with the relationship between the prominent frames at the top and bottom of the desk, marked respectively 5½″ and 7″. There is a mark which might indicate an uncertain height for the frame atop the switchboards. A similar uncertainty is evidenced about the link between the magnesite-faced desk and brick blocks. (Magnesite was a sound-absorbent mineral, mined in Greece, and applied extensively throughout the Larkin Building.)

The next elevation below shows the whole complex slightly narrowed in toward the center. Everything is more decisively drawn, particularly the extension of the switchboard panels beyond their brick piers, and instead of a

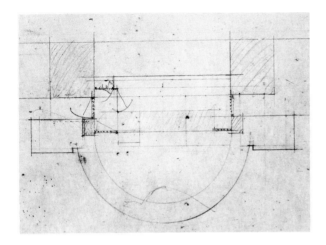

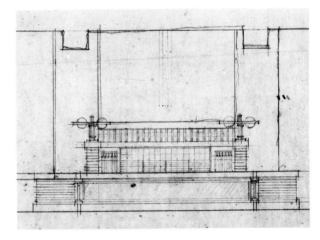

FIG. 43. Frank Lloyd Wright, second plan from studies in FIG. 39.

FIG. 44. Frank Lloyd Wright, first elevation from plan in FIG. 43.

plinth for a statue there now occurs an ornamental grated top, firmly framed. FIG. 42. This time the framing dimensions, reading down, are 7⅜″, 5″, 5″, and 7″. The elevator rails rise unmasked behind the switchboards.

The next (central) floor plan of the desk shows various doors to the interior as grates, and the space behind the switchboards has a door, perhaps indicating that the wall which shields the elevators houses equipment needing maintenance. FIG. 43. The elevation immediately below shows grated doors on either side of the switchboards; the plant bowls are eliminated. FIG. 44. The switchboard panel is extended to overlap the structural piers. Furthermore, there is some suggestion of a darker tonality on the curved face of the desk while its upper and lower frames remain light.

The lower elevation in this group reveals significant changes. A plinth atop the rear wall

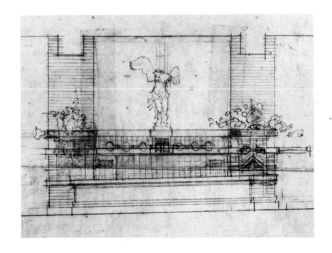

FIG. 45. Frank Lloyd Wright, second elevation from plan in FIG. 43.

now bears the unmistakable figure of the Winged Victory of Samothrace, while the rails rise behind her. FIG. 45. Her splendid forward

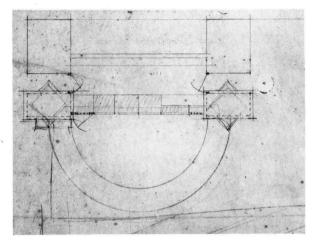

FIG. 46. Frank Lloyd Wright, third plan from studies in FIG. 39.

FIG. 47. Frank Lloyd Wright, perspective based on plan in FIG. 46.

FIG. 48. Frank Lloyd Wright, own house, Oak Park, Illinois, remodeled 1895, view into entry with ornamental frieze.

FIG. 49. Frank Lloyd Wright, Browne's bookstore, Chicago, 1908, with Victory of Samothrace.

movement and lift could be symbolic of the Larkin Company's advance. To either side, a plant bowl—whose top is level with the plinth —now aligns exactly with a structural pier. Lighting globes are strung above the switchboards and, on the right, more are roughed in below the planter. Wright has arrived at the emphatic terminals which would integrate the reception desk with the structure of the building.

The right-hand floor plan shows more ample space between telephone equipment and the wall behind the elevators and at last the desktop is wider. FIG. 46. At one end of the switchboards space is left (shown on other drawings) for a 'lightning accepter.'

The perspective drawing which closes this group fully presents the context in which the desk appears. FIG. 47. The brick blocks, reduced in plan, are higher. The Victory is set lower, level with the frames of the light fixtures.

This sheet of graphic exploration by Wright is so clearly sequential that one may imagine it done in a matter of hours, perhaps at night when all was quiet around him. The final result is amazing; he has taken a set of technological and human services and arranged them in what resembles an elaborate baroque altar. The celestial image is lifted above the center of a scrupulously detailed altar and flanked by rich arrangements of lights and verdure. One might ask how Wright had come to envisage the Victory of Samothrace as the focus of the composition. A cast of the Victory can be seen, about half the size sketched, in photographs of his own house, and there, too, he installed a spir-

FIG. 50.   Frank Lloyd Wright, Larkin Building front, 1904.

ited Hellenistic relief (cast in plaster and reduced in scale) around the frieze of his entry
hall. FIG. 48. There probably were distributors
of such classical embellishments.[3] As the Larkin
Building was nearing completion a small cast of
the Victory is shown in the interior of Browne's

bookstore designed by Wright. FIG. 49.
     Be all this as it may, there is a startling differ-
ence between the perspective sketch for the
desk and other symbolic and decorative details
of the Larkin Building. These fell into two separate groups— work done in collaboration with

FIG. 51.   Frank Lloyd Wright, Richard C. Bock, sculptures atop Larkin Building.

FIG. 52.   Frank Lloyd Wright, fountain at main entrance to Larkin Building; reliefs by Bock.

the Chicago sculptor Richard Bock, and abstract, geometric embellishments. On the exterior Bock's participation was displayed on the finials of slender, central piers on the north and south fronts. These piers carried eight bands (of terra-cotta?), atop the brickwork; higher still rose bold terrestrial globes signifying the commercial outreach of the Larkin Company. FIG. 50. These globes had clamps at each side, running far down and presumably into the brickwork. FIG. 51. At the top these clamps expanded into blocks clutched by unhappy waifs, their

arms and legs artificially forming x-shaped fences which could do nothing to restrain a globe were its clamps to give way. However, the best view may have been from the side as one walked along the street. Although these were unsuccessful works they introduced a theme which recurred in somewhat better arrangements—I mean the reliance on repeated, raised bands to associate the human figure with architecture. At the level of the finial bands mentioned above, short piers were sheathed in plaques of diagonal abstract pattern. The terra-

FIG. 53. Frank Lloyd Wright, Larkin Building, pier inside entrance.

cotta plaques also appeared on the side walls, and diagonal patterns recurred elsewhere.

Turning now to the bas-reliefs from which issued sheets of water, one finds allegorically garnished muses—tall, thin ladies with arms outstretched across the tops of inscribed tablets. FIG. 52. (Inscriptions outside and inside the Larkin Building have been carefully recorded by Quinan.) The muses had scrawny, semi-abstract arms, their garments were transformed into diagonal patterns. Behind them and their attributes (one even bore the helmet of Minerva) the same linear scoring will be found. Indoors, similar female figures, similarly clad, stood as guardian figures of the great fireplace. Behind them the scoring was like a sunburst; each figure was given unconvincing wings barely showing above its shoulders but counterbalancing the lines in back.

The uneasy mixture of Wright and Bock goes no farther here. At each end of the lobby fireplace wall two major structural piers were exceptionally crowned with clustered lamp globes and were decorated with softly toned, crisply rectangular bas-reliefs, differing noticeably from the bolder reliefs defining the central court of offices. FIGS. 53, 54. There, each pier displayed eight bands of intricate geometric motifs, apparently symbolizing the relentless repetition of machine parts. Facing the restaurant only a few of these motifs appeared. Similar mechanistic motifs do not seem to have recurred in Wright's works.

Thus the Larkin Building was ornamented by Bock's figures in the round and in bas-relief, then by two unrelated patterns of geometrical repetition, and still further, the sketch indicates, by a major symbol of Hellenistic derivation, entirely out of keeping with any of the above.

Now, however, the Larkin Company evidently introduced a strong new element into the reception-desk complex, one which drew power from the same area as did the elevators. Wright's own description of the intruder is quoted from Quinan's book:

Within the circular Information Desk, a prominent feature of the entrance lobby, are located telephone switchboards, with a capacity of 300 connections, the electrical Master Clock controlling the numerous secondary clocks and register clocks and automatically the signal gongs throughout the building, the switchboard by which the electrical time system is operated, and telegraph wires of both the Western Union and Postal Companies. FIGS. 37, 38.

It was the Master Clock which brought Wright back from the realms of symbolism to the new order of the machine age. The clock, backed by its 'synchronator,' shows on later plans. It is inched forward toward the desktop as far as possible and then given stepped-back corners and what appear to be ventilating openings at each side. Quinan's photographs indicate that the delicate balancing of bands was replaced by a forthright simplicity in the upper areas, then a strongly projecting edge of the desktop while the baseboard, just clear of the floor, is diminished. His photographs also show a small model of the Victory, looking vanquished on top of the Master Clock, then flying off to alight on a parapet of the restaurant floor — for how long one wonders. Did she perhaps

FIG. 54.   Frank Lloyd Wright, Larkin Building, piers in central court.

migrate to the more humane surroundings of Browne's book shop? Whatever her fate, Frank Lloyd Wright retrieved his control of the Larkin Building's expressive details as far as possible. He accepted the new order of the machine age with the brio it demanded and Bock's weaknesses subsided into relative modesty. Wright had created a great and original work of high architecture with masterful yet subtle spaces for the machine age, and carried it through in style. Understandably it became a cornerstone of his European reputation.

NOTES

1 *Frank Lloyd Wright's Larkin Building, Myth and Fact*, New York and Cambridge, Mass.: Architectural History Foundation and MIT Press, 1987.
2 Each globe contained, as Jack Quinan discovered, a 150-candlepower Nernst Glower, then considered the newest advance in artificial illumination.
3 Not yet identified.

Crisis and Creativity:
Frank Lloyd Wright, 1904–1914

I

What happens when creative work is crossed by personal crisis? Individual case histories, frequent enough in biographic literature, tend toward special pleading with scant factual evidence. It seemed possible to avoid these shortcomings, somewhat, while looking at the life and works of Frank Lloyd Wright around the time of his first marital break and first trip to Europe, 1909–1910. Wright's early architecture has been amply studied; disagreement about which of the buildings are capital achievements is slight. Many biographic data are known, and more were brought to light by Mrs. Linn Cowles, working in a Wright seminar at Columbia University. Her permission to use the new information is gratefully acknowledged.

Wright's personal crisis began to take shape with the Cheney commission of 1904; his life again changed radically after the tragic murder of Mrs. Cheney, his lover, and the destruction of his home in 1914; then new horizons were

Reprinted with changes from the *Journal of the Society of Architectural Historians,* December 1966.

indicated by the commission for the Imperial Hotel in Tokyo. Thus this investigation can cover a decade between the crucial actions.

What can be said after studying this record? The deployment of Wright's creativity continued despite personal travail and was only partially hindered by the pressure of public indignation. Mrs. Elizabeth Kassler pointed out to me that Wright was strengthened by an inner certainty that his course was, whatever people might say, profoundly moral; this is confirmed by evidence given below. One way or another, the tumultuous emotions, the large demonstrative acts, the catastrophe, slowed but did not stop or deflect the surge of Wright's art. The cost was bitter; Table 1 shows that Wright's commissions and the number of his executed works were about halved, comparing the span 1910–1914 with 1904–1909. Wright was to live through worse times and to suffer worse obloquy, but this mercifully he could not foresee.

II

In 1904 Wright completed the altogether extraordinary Larkin Administration Building

FRANK LLOYD WRIGHT WORKS 1904–1914

Public use, area plans, and service buildings.	Big houses and modest homes.
1904–1909:	
about 25 designs, 80% built.	about 70 designs, 60% built.
1910–1914:	
about 20 designs, 50% built	about 40 designs, 50% built.

TABLE 1. All figures rounded.

for the Martins in Buffalo; here Wright proved that the established Chicago style of commercial architecture no longer led the field. At the same time he created a splendid, almost equally free, city residence for D.D. Martin. FIG. 55. Three smaller residences of remarkable clarity were works of this year, too: the little Barton home annexed to the Martin; a project for a childhood friend, Robert Lamp; and the Cheney house that fatefully brought him and Mamah Borthwick Cheney together. FIG. 58.

Early in 1905 the Wrights and his clients of 1902, the Willetses, journeyed together to Japan. The Wrights' passports are dated 9 February as photostats supplied by Mr. Lloyd Wright indicate. Wright had been collecting Japanese prints for more than a decade; one shows in an obviously early interior of the Wright house with miscellaneous furniture. FIG. 56. The urge to visit Japan must have been strong, but perhaps there was also a need to think over the meaning of meeting Mrs. Cheney? The trip followed hard on the Cheney commission.

Later in 1905 two rather modest homes were built that have remained notable among Wright's designs. The Glasner house with complex, additive spaces in two stories included dining furniture within the living room area, a practice which became popular in small houses after World War I. The delightful Hardy House at Racine cascades in ingenious skip levels down an escarpment bordering Lake Michigan. In the same year Wright remodeled the main lobby space of the prominent Rookery Building in Chicago. Almost unnoticeably he built a small, concrete-framed factory for the E-Z Polish company, owned by the Martins. The 1905 factory showed that Wright had not lost his early interest in concrete, begun in the 1890s and evidenced in 1901 at an exposition building at Buffalo for the Universal Portland Cement Company, and a bank project published in *The Brick Builder*. FIGS. 59, 60. That same year the sixteen-story Ingalls Building in Cincinnati was begun, the highest reinforced-concrete-framed building in the United States. Wright may well have envied its daring while scorning its 'style.' At any rate, he introduced concrete into the Larkin Building only in precast parts—floor planks, stair stringers, and door frames. None of the commissions from the Martins gave scope to Wright's development of concrete as an architectural medium.

Wright then eagerly pursued this theme in Unity Temple, which started to rise by 1906 after long preparation. This building remained Wright's chief preoccupation until completed

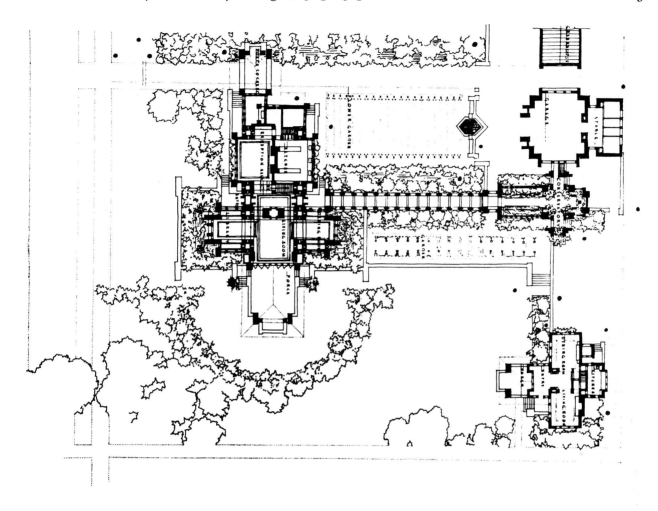

FIG. 55.   Frank Lloyd Wright, D.D. Martin residence and adjuncts, Buffalo, New York, 1904, plan.

in 1908. FIG. 61. Meanwhile, concrete was increasingly discussed because of its fireproof qualities which the disaster at San Francisco in 1906 underlined. Even Edison began experimenting, clumsily enough, with fireproof concrete prefabricated homes. Wright's version, published in *The Ladies' Home Journal* (and actually built in cheaper materials), was a simple but elegant cubic structure. FIG. 57. He then reworked a project for a small apartment building designed for Warren McArthur. In 1907 a masterful residential project for the Harold F.

FIG. 56.   Frank Lloyd Wright, own house, Oak Park, Illinois, interior ca. 1887. Japanese print atop upright piano, left side.

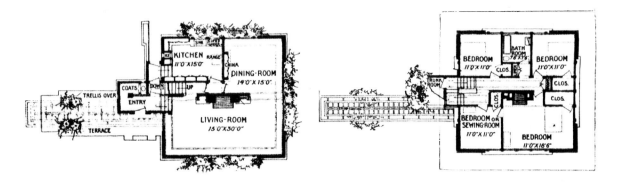

FIG. 57. Frank Lloyd Wright, project for a fireproof house in concrete, for the Curtis Publishing Company, 1906.

FIG. 58. Frank Lloyd Wright, Edwin H. Cheney house, Oak Park, Illinois, 1904.

FIG. 59.   Frank Lloyd Wright, Universal Portland Cement Company display at the Pan-American Exposition, Buffalo, New York, 1901.

McCormicks united an elaborate pavilion scheme recalling Japanese palaces, but with the security of concrete. Wright's design was rejected by Mrs. McCormick, the former Edith Rockefeller (later so attached to Jung). This did not discourage other wealthy clients like the Avery Coonleys. Their ethereally lovely house, opened in 1908, was the masterwork of Wright's architecture in those years. FIG. 63. The ingenious Robie House, heavily dramatic, was created in 1909, the year in which Wright reportedly failed to secure Henry Ford as a client. (Edsel Ford might have arranged a meeting of the two men.) Wright's marital troubles and

FIG. 60.   Frank Lloyd Wright, early study, concrete monolith bank, 1894, *Brick Builder,* August 1901.

professional discontents were about to lead to his sensational elopement with Mamah Borthwick Cheney.

III

Wright's fiber as a man and as an architect was tested to the full by this dramatic move. His wife, Catherine, refused to grant him a divorce, and his six children were subjected to harsh strains. Mr. Cheney immediately gave his wife a divorce, and custody of their children was divided between them. What might Anna Wright, the divorced mother of the architect,

FIG. 61.   Frank Lloyd Wright, Unity Temple, Oak Park, Illinois, 1906–8.

have thought of all this? We do not know. She had lived next door to her son and his family in Oak Park, and she remained close to him throughout her life. Through her the Lloyd Joneses were Wright's family.

Wright was forty-two years old when he abandoned family and career, as family documents now at Avery Library, Columbia University, make clear. He had a world to lose. He had enlarged his home with a children's playroom where Froebel instruction was imparted, and probably it was Anna Wright, trained teacher and Froebel enthusiast who—at the beginning at least—dominated there. FIG. 62. Wright had contributed to her livelihood since he began to earn his way. In 1909 Wright could count on her, and a few others of his family, as well as on Mamah Borthwick, and he was working on a monumental and handsome publication of his architecture, issued in Berlin in 1911. It was his work and even more the development of his work, that Wright cared for above all things and people. He was not a family man, despite progeny and relatives.

FIG. 62.   Frank Lloyd Wright, own house, Oak Park, Illinois, playroom added about 1905.

His elopement was inexplicable in terms normally accepted in his community and times. Wright tried more than once with only negative results to clarify his concept of a morality higher than that sanctioned by both church and state. But in 1912 he and Mamah Borthwick jointly published a translation of a brief treatise by Ellen Key, a well-known Swedish feminist, entitled *Love and Ethics*. It cost one dollar, and said more simply what he believed. We read:

Not the marriage service, but the will of two people to bear the responsibility of their children; not the "legitimacy" of the children, but their quality; [these] be the standard of value for the morality of parenthood....All these new principles require an organic growth of duty together with happiness, an increase of responsibility...erotic happiness becomes a vital social value....Happiness is...in its deepest sense the enhancement of life through the vicissitudes of life. And in the deepest sense also does happiness become the sacred duty of one who sees the aim of life in life itself....Life is no *made* thing but a *becoming,* with unsuspected possibilities.

FIG. 63.   Frank Lloyd Wright, Coonley house, Riverside, Illinois, 1907–10.

Were these phrases put forth to justify indulgences already three years old? There is no reason to think so. The famous trip to Europe was hardly an illicit honeymoon. There was much work to be done on the publication by Ernst Wasmuth. Wright's son Lloyd was there to help him. He later wrote to Mrs. Cowles:

Then came the break-up of the Oak Park family life, with the advent of Mamah Borthwick, and the building of the first Taliesin in the Spring Green valley on the Wisconsin River. My brother John, and myself, were attending Wisconsin University in 1909, where I had gone to prepare myself to be an architect and landscape architect so that I could assist in my father's work. The rest of the children were with Mother in the Oak Park home...

The House of Wasmuth had approached Frank Lloyd Wright about producing a monograph of his work....Father had gone to Germany that fall with Mamah Borthwick to see what the project might entail and to escape the news hounds' rabble-feeding persecution. It was a difficult and crucial time for all of us. After some time, in Germany, Father wired funds for me to join him in Italy. A draughtsman who had been in his employ for several years named [Taylor] Wooley was already there. A sensitive draughtsman, a Mormon from Salt Lake City, who though lame, was active, helpful, and a hard worker.

Though this work in Italy would break into my college year of 1910, Father felt the experience would be worth it to me in more ways than one—it was indeed!

I found Father already established in the little

FIG. 64.   Frank Lloyd Wright, playhouse on the Coonley estate, Riverside, Illinois, 1912.

Villino "Fortuna" just below the piazzale Michelangelo and the David statue—in Florence....The villino was divided into two parts opening from a tiny inner court....We had the street apartment.... There were no rugs on the stone floor and it was cold. The three of us set up our tables in the living-room and brought in braziers to warm the room and our freezing hands for it was the end of the winter season and we had to thaw out to do the essential and delicate work.

Father had had shipped to him all of the drawings from Taliesin and the Chicago office that he planned to include in the brochure on his work. It was a mixed lot of water colors by various Chicago men, line drawings by Marion Mahoney and other draughtsmen in the office, and his own renderings and sketches which showed the influence of two very different sources—the Japanese prints and the pen drawings filled with sunlight, by [Daniel Urrabieta] Vierge. These, together with Father's own typical expression, created a type of rendering unique to itself and its creator, Frank Lloyd Wright. It was ideally suited to convey a record of his work.

This work had to be done quickly and all correlated, reconstructed, and prepared for the Wasmuth edition. We worked long and continuously.

Father, Wooley, and I traced with crow quill pens on tracing paper, all of the drawings and matters he wished to have published in the brochure. We worked at modifying, building up, correcting, simplifying, and converting all of the material into the totally coordinated plates that were reproduced for the *Ausgeführte Bauten und Entwürfe von Frank Lloyd Wright,* by Wasmuth in Germany.

During the several months we were engaged in this work he returned several times for several days at a time, to Germany to consult with the Wasmuth concern about the publication, and to see Mamah Borthwick who had stayed behind in Germany.... He said nothing about lectures there....This was father's first trip to Europe; he wrote his English texts. He could not speak German. I do not know who made the German translation...

It took high concentration, time, and application of an intense order to turn out the work, under the circumstances....After we completed the drawings of the plates, they were taken to Germany and lithographic stones were there prepared from them.

The work done, Father gave Wooley and me a stake with which to "do" Italy to study the gardens, urban plans and great art works of the country. We travelled third class from the top to the toe of Italy, drinking in the wonders with the help of youth and Asti Spumante....Wooley then went back to Salt Lake City, where he was to distribute the *Sonderheft* [a smaller book of photographs, not the portfolios] in the Western States. I returned through France, where I met Father in Paris for a good visit.

Because of my interest in landscape architecture, we went to see the gardens of Versailles and several chalets. Then followed the Tuileries, seeing the treasures of the Louvre, and the Folies-Bergère, and the night life of Paris. Then we spent a day at the then growing airport of Le Bourget. I wanted to see the Bleriot monoplane and what they were doing in France in aerodynamics. I had invented a delta wing plane remarkably like those of today....Father encouraged me in my interest...

Our work and travelling accomplished, Father then joined Mamah Borthwick in Fiesole, where they stayed for several months....before returning to Taliesin in Wisconsin.

These excerpts illuminate vividly an important passage in Wright's life. Moreover they may confirm Wright's own phrases about the first Taliesin: "That spring of 1909...I turned to this hill" and "Taliesin withstood five years" until it was burned in 1914. The first Taliesin, whenever completed, might have been put to use before Wright left for Europe in 1909.[1]

IV

After he returned, by 1911, he and Mamah Borthwick lived at Taliesin, and Wright kept an office in Chicago as well. The Coonleys came to him for a variety of improvements to their estate. The principal one was the small playhouse, in reality a kindergarten where Mrs. Coonley could put to use some of the ideas suggested by John Dewey. The Coonley playhouse was a miniature masterwork; it contained Wright's fully developed abstract color compositions in windows. FIG. 64. Though created as architectural supplements, these are self-contained artistic exercises which match the dates of the early abstract designs by European painters—Kupka, Larionov, Delaunay, Kandinsky.

When the playhouse opened Wright was busy with a project for a concrete-framed skyscraper, half again as tall as the Ingalls Building. FIG. 65. This was for the *San Francisco Call*. FIG. 66. Wright's models show the first slab skyscraper, slenderly elegant and beautifully articulated. Unlike some other towers, this was not slim because it rose from a mere sliver of real estate, but because its form neatly evolved from a spine of elevators. Wright advanced commercial building to a new stage, though his project remained unbuilt. So too remained his best de-

FIG. 65. Elzner and Anderson, Ingalls Building, Cincinnati, 1903. A National Historical Civil Engineering Landmark since 1974. "This first skyscraper of reinforced concrete was carefully built, a floor slab every twelve days, to the unheard of height of sixteen stories. The patented Ransome system was employed, wherein steel bars, stirrups and hoops provided the essential shear and tensile reinforcement. . . . Skeptical city building officials delayed the project two years before approving the design." (The Architectural Foundation of Cincinnati, *Architecture and Construction in Cincinnati*, 1987.)

FIG. 66. Frank Lloyd Wright, project for a building for the *San Francisco Call*, 1912.

signs for entire communities and for small and large houses in the years 1910–1914.

In 1913 Wright began to design Midway Gardens, a large elaborate restaurant with rooms for special events. FIGS. 67, 68. It was nearly complete when it opened in August 1914—a sparkling mixture of Wright's fresh ideas and insights. Around the central garden symmetrical groupings of pavilions, balconies, and tur-

FIG. 67.   Frank Lloyd Wright, Midway Gardens, Chicago, Illinois, 1914, decorative mural.

FIG. 68.   Frank Lloyd Wright, Midway Gardens, sculpture as a pivot for space.

rets, in brick partly decorated with concrete plaques, rose and fell like the waves of music that enlivened them as much as did the abstract murals and semiabstract sculptures that Wright freely introduced. The murals extended the ideas of the Coonley playhouse windows; the statues were close to those Josef Hoffmann had used in the Kunstschau of 1908. Wright could easily have seen them either reproduced or in reality; he visited central Europe during his trip especially to see the works of the Secessionist architects, Wagner, Olbrich, and Hoffmann. Midway Gardens has been recognized as one of Wright's most stimulating works.

When Midway Gardens was nearly ready to open Wright learned that Taliesin had been set on fire, and that Mamah Borthwick, her two children, and four others had been murdered by a berserk houseman. The tragedy has been told, in all its implications, by Wright in *An Autobiography*. With incredible courage he set about rebuilding his home. The first approaches had already been made to him by representatives from Japan, seeking an architect for a quasi-official hotel next to the Emperor's palace gardens in Tokyo. When, in later years,

Wright talked of "snatching victory from the jaws of defeat" it was more than a phrase on his lips.

SOURCES USED

Maginel Wright Barney, *The Valley of the God-almighty Joneses;* Mary Ellen Chase, *A Goodly Fellowship;* Finis Farr, *Frank Lloyd Wright;* Henry-Russell Hitchcock, *In The Nature of Materials;* Grant Manson, *Frank Lloyd Wright to 1910, the First Golden Age;* Frank Lloyd Wright, *An Autobiography,* 1932; John Lloyd Wright, *My Father Who Is On Earth;* and for the Larkin Building, *The Empire State Architect* for 1947 and 1950.

NOTE

1 In 1985 Walter Creese reported that the Iowa County Registry of Deeds at Dodgeville, Wisconsin, shows that Wright's mother "bought...land...from Josep Rieder on April 10, 1911, for $2274.88" in *The Crowning of the American Landscape: eight great spaces and their buildings,* 252, n.18

Frank Lloyd Wright's Years of Modernism, 1925–1935

Through almost five years, 1925–1929, the very air Frank Lloyd Wright breathed was thick with catastrophe. His home, Taliesin, was once again destroyed by fire. Debts drove him to the verge of bankruptcy. Hysterical persecutions by his former mistress, Miriam Noel, plagued him and the new family who were to remain close to him through the rest of his life. These black years were survived only by means of personal love and consciousness of creative achievement. This achievement had just been recorded in 1925 on the sumptuous pages of the Dutch publication, *Wendigen.* Soon, at the urging of his wife, Olgivanna, Wright started to evoke his childhood, beginning *An Autobiography.*

Unsurprisingly, the architectural yield of these years is strange and ideal, especially in contrast to the immediate past when Wright had built the lavish Hollyhock House and more compact concrete block houses for Mrs. Millard, John Storer, the Ennises, and the Freemans (FIGS. 69–72), all in California, and had

Reprinted with changes from the *Journal of the Society of Architectural Historians,* March 1965.

FIG. 69. Frank Lloyd Wright, Millard house, Pasadena, California, 1923.

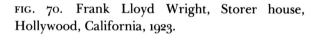

FIG. 70. Frank Lloyd Wright, Storer house, Hollywood, California, 1923.

FIG. 71. Frank Lloyd Wright, Ennis house, Hollywood, California, 1924.

planned elaborate projects for A.M. Johnson, an adventuresome insurance magnate, in Chicago and in Death Valley. FIG. 73. Building little, he surveyed various avenues which were to lead to major achievements. And, perhaps due to the extravagant coterie centered on the mistress of Hollyhock House, Wright became an advocate of the idealist modernism we recognize as typical of the 1920s: worldwide horizons, technological miracles, the thrill of speed, the challenge of untried potentials. This view of Wright's work at this time was indicated by Henry-Russell Hitchcock, but has been little examined since.

In 1925 and 1926 two dreams arose in Wright's mind, the Gordon Strong Planetarium and Automobile Objective, and the Steel Interfaith Cathedral. FIGS. 74, 75. Both projects celebrated

modern technology with, for Wright, unprecedented vigor.

At the crest of Sugar Loaf, a 1,200-foot mountain some thirty miles northwest of Washington, D.C., Wright proposed a planetarium, then the newest symbol of the popular appeal of science— Zeiss had just opened theirs at Jena to international applause. Around the required dome Wright spiraled a broad roadway to a platform commanding views of the Potomac valley and the Catoctin range. Motoring was coming of age; over smooth highways created by the expanding economy after World War I sped new, small family cars and the sleek, roaring imports of sporty enthusiasts. Wright projected an ideal excursion for them.

Less specifically considered, the vast glass pyramid of the Interfaith Cathedral was to rise,

FIG. 72.   Frank Lloyd Wright, Freeman house, Hollywood, California, 1924.

braced by steel, as high as Sugar Loaf and its superstructure, a 1,500-foot man-made summit, the highest ever. Like Bruno Taut a decade earlier, it would seem Wright was conjecturing some kind of 'alpine architecture.'

The formal elements of these two projects recur in some of Wright's later, freest works of the 1940s and 1950s. Circles, triangles, polyhedra rose openly from their long abeyence in Wright's ornamental details and romantic roofs to become focuses of his architectural thought. Wright's once eloquently shaped roofs had dwindled to invisibility in the California block

structures. But, in a reversal typical of him, roofs again dominated walls in the tepee-play of the Nakoma and Tahoe projects, 1922 and 1924. FIGS. 76, 78. By 1926 such Indianizing was absorbed into the superhuman scale and sheer crystallinity of the cathedral.

In 1928 Wright began to consider his projects for the resort called San Marcos in the Desert, near Chandler, Arizona; a large hotel and private villas were planned. FIG. 77. Living near the site, Wright became fascinated with the triangular forms nature presented in the landscape, flora, and fauna there. The triangle now ap-

FIG. 73. Frank Lloyd Wright, project for National Life Insurance Building, Chicago, Illinois, 1924.

peared, not in roof or silhouette as before, but as the module of plan and elevation, sharply responsive to sun and shade—the source of shimmer typical of desert landscape. The free movement of the 30-degree angle in plan was consciously explored. In time, it would yield a grammar for some of Wright's most intriguing and livable works.

The 1928 projects were developed in a temporary camp called Ocotilla (after the ocotillo cactus) where rough lumber and canvas flaps were used, as later in the original structure of Taliesin West. FIG. 79. Transcontinental jour-

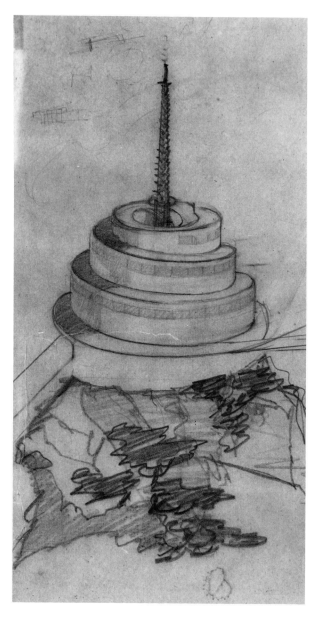

FIG. 74. Frank Lloyd Wright, project for the Gordon Strong Automobile Objective on Sugar Loaf mountain, Maryland, 1925.

FIG. 75.   Frank Lloyd Wright, project for a 1,500-foot-high Steel Cathedral, 1926.

FIG. 76.   Frank Lloyd Wright, project for Nakoma Country Club, Madison, Wisconsin, 1924.

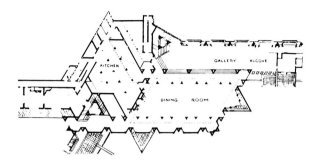

FIG. 77.   Frank Lloyd Wright, project for San Marcos in the Desert, near Chandler, Arizona, 1927, upper main rooms of hotel.

neys to and from Wisconsin by car of course meant more to Wright than his earlier seasick crossings of the Pacific. The automobile assumed great importance in his concepts, and soon he began to develop ideas for motor courts and service stations (FIGS. 80, 81), crisp, modern architecture for grass-roots Americans.

The year 1929 opened well for Wright. The *Architectural Record* had welcomed him to its pages month after month, and the San Marcos projects were brilliantly developed. The small but influential congregation of St. Mark's in the Bouwerie was considering his most advanced ideas of apartment buildings for New York City where he had never built before. FIG. 84. Wright had on the boards different and ingenious ideas for an apartment block commissioned by Elizabeth Noble in Los Angeles. FIG. 82. But it was the St. Mark's towers which advanced his structural concepts, no doubt in consultation with his regular engineer, Paul Mueller, far beyond the insurance company project of 1924.

In 1929 Wright was still able to demonstrate his most complete transformation of the wall in

FIG. 78.   Frank Lloyd Wright, project for summer colony at Lake Tahoe, California, 1922.

FIG. 79.   Frank Lloyd Wright, Ocotilla desert camp, near Chandler, 1927.

FIG. 80.   Frank Lloyd Wright, project for San Marcos Water Gardens, near Chandler, 1927.

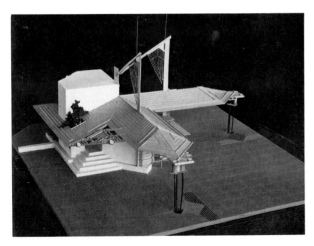

FIG. 81. Frank Lloyd Wright, project for small service station, 1928.

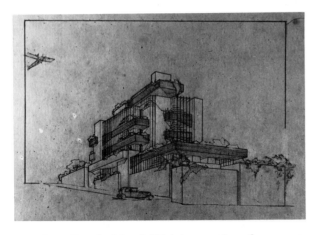

FIG. 82. Frank Lloyd Wright, project for apartments in Los Angeles for Elizabeth Noble, 1929.

a house constructed for his cousin, Richard Lloyd Jones, a newspaper publisher in Tulsa. FIG. 83. Regularly alternating vertical piers and glass strips, equally wide, enclosed the home and its annexes without a hint of roof. Usually

criticized for its exterior, the same pier device in the interior yielded delightful spaces. The exterior surpasses a somewhat similar pattern used for Raymond Hood's Daily News skyscraper in New York, 1930, which presented a far greater opportunity.

Then, the stock market crash. Wright's commissions vanished. The year 1930 brought only the Kahn lectures at Princeton, published the following year as *Modern Architecture*. (The word *modern* was in the air; in 1929 the Museum of Modern Art had been founded in New York.)

Again, 1931 brought purely ideal notions of Wright to paper. Two out of three seem disappointing. The skyscraper schemes offer little but gigantic, picturesque glassiness and ornament hardly better than the imitation-Wright ornament Peter Behrens had occasionally used for exhibition work in 1924 and 1925. FIG. 85. The House on the Mesa, a project which Wright exhibited in 1932 at the Museum of Modern Art, had a daring cantilever over the open swimming pool, recalling the extended free horizontals of Mies's 1924 project for a reinforced-concrete country house. FIG. 86. But in many sketches for The House on the Mesa only the living room roof is cantilevered and the counterbalancing extension over the pool is omitted. The result is cold, almost like Perret's works, perhaps because of the module which rigidly governs both plan and elevation. Of all this only the stepped-in windows were salvaged in Wright's later work, the Walker House at Carmel.

A third 1931 project was a modest proposal for a newspaper plant in Salem, Oregon. FIG. 87. It presented the seed idea of the Johnson Wax administration block built in Racine—hollow,

FIG. 83.   Frank Lloyd Wright, Richard Lloyd Jones house, Tulsa, Oklahoma, 1929.

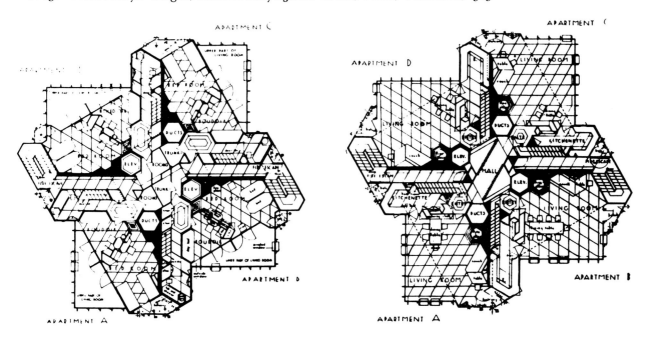

FIG. 84.   Frank Lloyd Wright, project for St. Mark's apartments, New York, New York, 1929.

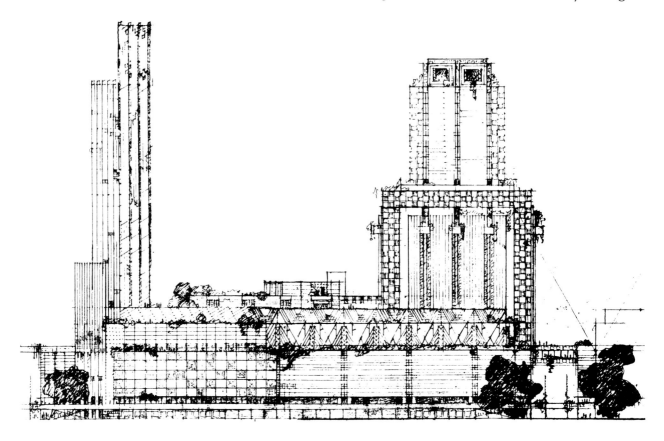

FIG. 85.   Frank Lloyd Wright, project for set-back skyscrapers, 1931.

FIG. 86.   Frank Lloyd Wright, project for a House on the Mesa, 1931.

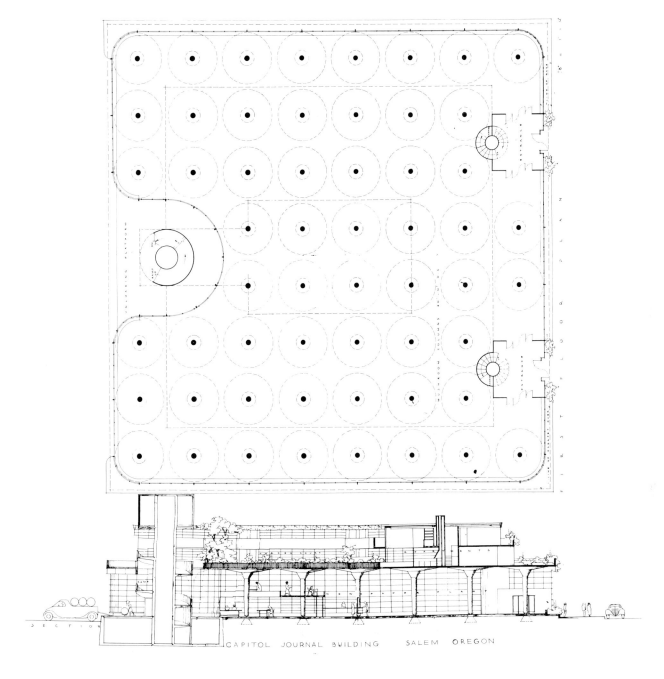

FIG. 87.   Frank Lloyd Wright, project for the Capital Journal building, Salem, Oregon, 1931.

FIG. 88.   Frank Lloyd Wright, project for the Davidson Sheet Steel farm buildings, 1932.

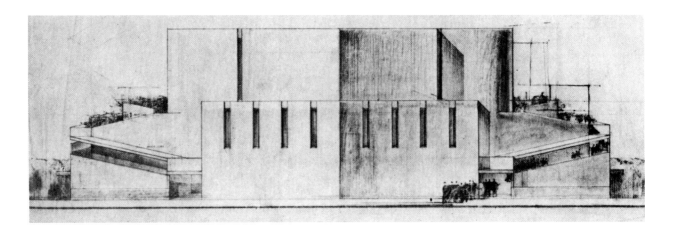

FIG. 89.   Frank Lloyd Wright, project for the New Theatre, 1932.

tapered, wide-capped columns with skylights between. Here Wright envisioned a dissolution of the roof as drastic as that of the wall at the Lloyd Jones house.

In 1932 Wright's grip on modernism, as defined above, was steady. Various, largely unconventional, ideas for theaters which he had assembled over the years were reworked and integrated into a project called The New Theatre, substantially that built late in Wright's life at Dallas. FIG. 89. Prefabricated farm buildings, stamped in quantity like automobile bodies, and related roadside markets (foreshadowing shopping marts) were designed for Walter Davidson. FIG. 88. Cantilevering was modestly reintroduced in a project for Dean Malcolm Willey of Minneapolis, a relaxed adaptation of a 1925 project for Mrs. Gladney. FIG. 90.

My rather grudging attitude toward Wright's architectural projects of the Depression years is inapplicable to the romantic autobiography he published in 1932. Started at his wife's urging, it has some of the poetic outlook of Louis Sullivan's *Autobiography of an Idea.* Wright's *An Autobiography,* together with the 1932 founding of the Taliesin Fellowship, demonstrates Wright's creative resourcefulness even in the least promising circumstances. Long after most Wright buildings will have been razed the original text of his biography should carry his spirit to new generations. The other book he published in 1932, *The Disappearing City,* was unsatisfactory and he rewrote it twice, yet it launched him on the Broadacre City scheme which has continued to challenge planning specialists over the years.

Despite minimal resources, facilities for the Taliesin Fellowship were under way in 1933. A large drafting room and dormitories were added to the remodeled Home School originally designed for his aunts in 1902. The wide-trussed drafting room added vigor to the extended Taliesin complex. FIG. 91.

The winter of 1933–1934 was spent mainly on the Broadacre model and models of some of its components at larger scale. FIG. 92. All were

FIG. 90. Frank Lloyd Wright, project for the Malcolm Willey house, 1932.

shown first in New York at Radio City, then elsewhere in the United States. To a general public, bewildered and deprived by the Great Depression, this presented a vision of a good life unlike any previously experienced. But its ideas played no roles in the reconstruction which pulled America out of the trough. A more modest house than that first proposed was built in 1934 for the Willeys—the first commission by others than himself and his family designed and executed by Wright since the Freeman house in Los Angeles, ten long years before.

In 1935 Wright designed a daring project for Mary and Stanley Marcus of Dallas: a crisp, roomy house sheltered under a single, generous envelope of insect screening. Mrs. Marcus liked screens at the windows.

Thereafter, modernism contributed to Frank Lloyd Wright's familiar masterworks of the later 1930s, but it was no longer the dominant characteristic it had been. No doubt the change is due to some degree to the difference between real construction and paper fantasies. But even more it is due to the continuing matu-

FIG. 91.   Frank Lloyd Wright, Hillside drafting room, near Spring Green, Wisconsin, 1933.

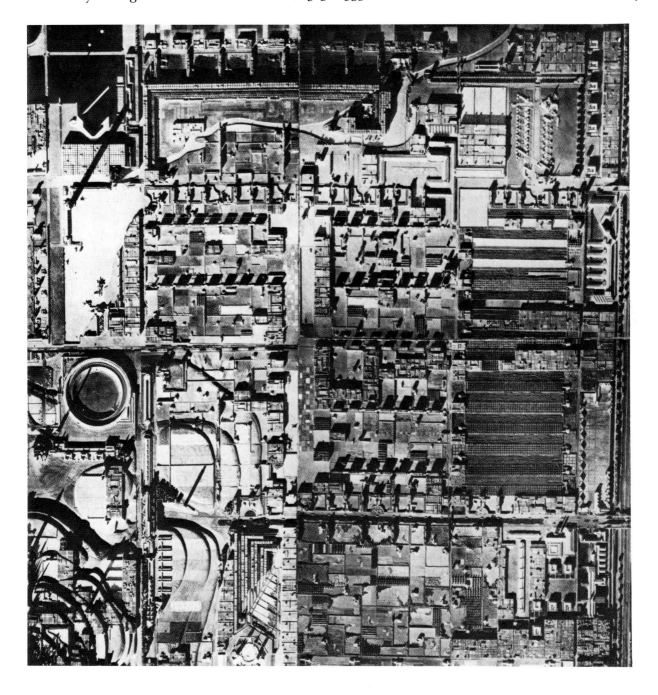

FIG. 92. Frank Lloyd Wright, project for Broadacre City, a model, 1934.

ration of Wright's genius. The automobile, pre-fabrication, one-worldism, and new-worldism were elements of his thinking rather than the leitmotifs of his designs after 1934. Falling-water, the Johnson administrative complex, the Hanna house, the first Jacobs house, Taliesin West, and Florida Southern College brought Wright into a deeper and wider response to the nature of architecture.

Frank Lloyd Wright:
Plasticity, Continuity, and Ornament

In 1928–1929 Frank Lloyd Wright went into the Arizona desert with a crew of assistants to plan a great resort complex for Alexander Chandler. FIG. 93. Wright's wife, Olgivanna, and their small daughters went with him. He devised ingenious structures in rough boarding and doubled canvas flaps to house this group temporarily in the wilds. Exhilarated by his environment, Wright took new bearings on architecture. As he motored across the vast expanses of the West he saw in the highways and gas stops the framework of future decentralized communities. FIG. 95. How would architecture evoke the poetry of this new American pattern? In the mountains, the cacti, and the desert fauna Wright discovered angularities, combinations of 30, 60, and 120 degrees, offering supple patterns of movement and repose. FIG. 94. These patterns might be traced in dotted sequences of solid material through which space permeated freely, a device Wright had used only sparingly before. These elements together with his novel inexpensive building system of reinforced-con-

crete shells suggested to Wright the outline of a grand architectural potential. The euphoria was brief; by the end of 1929 the market crash and the onset of the Depression stopped everything short. Abetted by his wife Wright took to writing and lecturing as a way of life. Already in his sixties, he found people, especially young architects, interested more in what he had accomplished and experienced than in his unfulfilled dreams. Wright recounted his start amid Queen Annery and imperial plaster classicism, then the dawn of clarity in the Prairie School works, leading to his more advanced achievements in Japan and California.

However, Wright felt he should be drawing and building, not talking and writing, and even more he felt that to freeze concepts in verbal formulas would harm his greatest resource, imagination. Wright's statements have character and direction, but he often obscured the underlying thought in turgid, inconsistent phrasing. Nevertheless these early texts reveal Wright's architectural development; how his insight grew can be demonstrated in his own words. I shall attempt this briefly with two of Wright's more puzzling words, *plasticity* and

Reprinted from the *Journal of the Society of Architectural Historians*, March 1978.

FIG. 93.   Frank Lloyd Wright, project for San Marcos in the Desert, 1927.

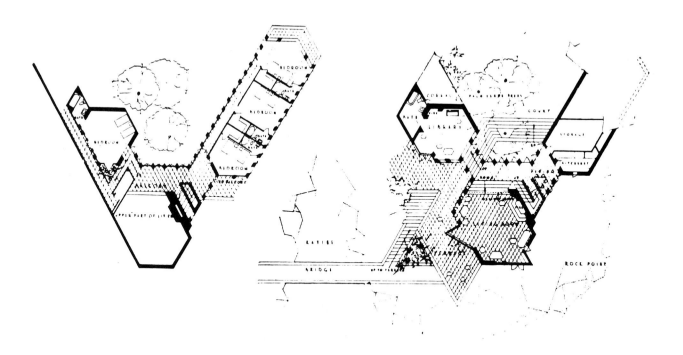

FIG. 94.   Frank Lloyd Wright, project for the Cudney house, San Marcos in the Desert, near Chandler, Arizona, 1927.

continuity, often used interchangeably by him, but in the long run conveying a transition from one stage of architectural understanding to another more mature one. As the concepts become disentangled another aspect of Wright's work, his ornament, long misunderstood, will appear in its original significance.

The quotations are taken from Wright's publications of the 1930s: lectures at the Art Institute of Chicago and at Princeton; *An Autobiography;* and articles in the Madison, Wisconsin, *Capital Times.*[1] Wright's basic texts may well reach back to 1926 or 1927 when he started *An*

FIG. 95.   Frank Lloyd Wright and his family motoring in the desert, 1928.

FIG. 96.   Frank Lloyd Wright, dining area in living room, Taliesin, near Spring Green, Wisconsin, ca. 1916.

Autobiography. To begin with plasticity:

Plasticity was a familiar term but something I had seen in no building whatsoever. I had seen it in Lieber Meister's ornament only; it had not found its way into his buildings otherwise.[2] It might now be seen gradually coming into the expressive lines and surfaces of the buildings I was building.[3]

Wright then turns to the importance of machine production in accord with the stand he had taken in "The Art and Craft of the Machine," 1901.[4]

The machine resources were so little understood that extensive drawings had to be made merely to show the "mill-man" what to leave off. But the "trim" finally became only a...flat, narrow...wood band...around the room....[5] [FIG. 96].

I did make the "trim" plastic,...continuously flowing, instead of the prevailing heavy "cut and butt" carpenter work....[FIG. 98]. The machine could do it all perfectly well as I laid it out.[6]

When the interior had thus become wholly plastic ...a new element...entered architecture. Strangely enough an element that had not existed...before... this revolutionary sense of the plastic whole, an instinct with me at first, began to work more and more intelligently and have fascinating, unforeseen consequences.[7]

Perhaps the most remarkable consequence can be seen in Wright's treatment of the piers inside Unity Temple. At first each pier was to be ornamented elaborately and equally on all four faces. The final decision was to use a simple band of dark wood defining color fields wrapped around the two interior faces of each pier.[8] FIGS. 97, 99. Thus the ornament which originally emphasized the entity of each pier came to accent the importance of the central space. This was Wright's clear declaration of the primacy of space over matter.

Now why not let walls, ceilings, floors become *seen* as component parts of each other, their surfaces flowing into each other.[9] [FIG. 100]...why not throw away entirely all implications of post and beam construction? Have no posts, no columns, no pilasters, cornices or moldings or ornament; no divisions of the sort nor allow any fixtures whatever to enter as something added to the structure. Any building would be complete, including all within itself. Instead of many things *one* thing. I promoted plasticity as conceived by Lieber Meister to *continuity* in the concept of the building as a whole.[10]

Wright next explains how working 'in the nature of materials'[11] facilitates continuity.

Glass as we use it now is a miracle. Air to keep air out or keep it in. Light itself in light, to diffuse or reflect, or refract light itself....[12] Open reaches of the ground may enter...the building and the building interior may reach out and associate with...the ground. Ground and building will thus become more and more...directly related to each other in oneness and intimacy. Walls...because of glass will become windows and windows as...holes in walls will be seen no more. Ceilings will often become as window-walls too. Sunlit space...becomes the servant of...the human spirit.[13]

Of course...primitive post-and-beam construction will always be valid, but both support and supported may by means of...welded steel...or...woven filaments of steel and modern concrete castings be...united as one physical body: ceilings and walls made...into one another. This Continuity is made possible by the tenuity of steel....The cantilever is the simplest one of the important phases of this ... new structural resource....It has yet had little attention in architecture. It can do remarkable things to liberate space.[14] [FIG. 101].

Indeed, an earlier author admired by Emerson, E.L. Garbett, in his *Rudimentary Treatise on the Principles of Design in Architecture*, 1850, had predicted that tensile construction (in his day limited to trusses and braced frames) would give rise to 'the architecture of the future.'[15] The *Treatise* was reissued often. If Wright did not know Garbett's ideas first-hand he probably encountered them among the thoughts of friends and associates in the early days in Chicago.

Now, Wright leads smoothly from the nature of materials to what he calls nature-pattern, that is, the pattern latent in a material and in its appropriate use.

...as many fascinating...properties as there are different materials...will...naturally qualify, modify, and utterly change all architectural form...the architect must begin again at the very beginning... now he must sensibly go through with whatever material may be at hand...according to the methods and sensibilities of a man in this age....I mean inherent *structure* seen always by the architect as a matter of complete design. It is in itself, always, *nature-pattern*. It is this profound internal sense of materials that enters in as Architecture now....Heretofore, I have used the word "pattern" instead of the word ornament to avoid confusion or to escape the passing prejudice. But here now ornament is in its place.

Ornament meaning not only *surface qualified by human imagination* but imagination giving *natural pattern* to structure. [FIG. 102]. Perhaps this phrase says it all without further explanation.[16]

It has been possible to trace Wright's growing awareness of the power of continuity, first on surfaces, then in structure, in space, and in the expression of these architectural factors working together. Wright begins this development with the plastic ornament fluently created by his master, Louis Sullivan, and terminates it with his own quite different sense of ornament as the requisite refinement of the natural pattern of structure.

Wright's ornament (in architectural trim, art-glass windows, furniture, and other decorative adjuncts) usually is trivial when isolated. It reaches significance as the obbligato accompaniment to some specific architectural composition that Wright was orchestrating. Then it takes its place in Wright's prolonged search for ever more inclusive continuity.

What led Wright into this preoccupation with continuity? I believe he saw human life as one of the processes of nature, not as some exceptional form of creation. Within nature people are active, adapting nature to suit their wants; they contribute feedback within the natural system. Similarly, he saw architecture as a natural process of human life, in turn nourishing its parent system. Thus to Wright architecture, humankind, and nature were joined in a grand dynamic continuity, and continuity within architecture indicated that people were aligning themselves—as he believed they should—with the natural forces of life.

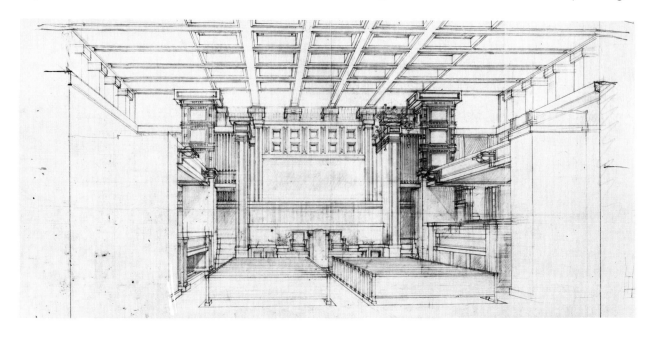

FIG. 97. Frank Lloyd Wright, study for the interior of Unity Temple, ca. 1906. Four great piers, which included heating ducts, support a roof of crossed reinforced concrete beams closed by lay lights beneath a skylight. The interior side walls rise to clearstory strips, avoiding the expression of support. Here, piers are lavishly decorated equally on each of four sides.

FIG. 98. Arthur Little, 1880–81, cut-and-butt wood trim.

FIG. 99.   Frank Lloyd Wright, interior view of Unity Temple as completed 1908. Plain, dark wood strips and tinted wall planes now are oriented in toward the central space. This ornament opened a new emphasis on space, hitherto explored only in special features (like the Martin House gallery [FIG. 55]). Eventually, plain ornament itself ceded way to the expressive handling of structural materials (as in FIG. 102).

FIG. 100.   Frank Lloyd Wright, Guggenheim Museum, New York, New York, interior, 1959.

FIG. 101. Frank Lloyd Wright, Fallingwater, Mill Run, Pennsylvania, terrace of guest wing, 1939.

FIG. 102. Frank Lloyd Wright, Fallingwater, Mill Run, Pennsylvania, stone and glass junction, 1937.

NOTES

1 Compare this to Wright's earlier use of decorative plaques in the Larkin Building and Midway Gardens. Quotations are taken from four sources: (a) *Two Lectures on Architecture*, Chicago, 1931; (b) *Modern Architecture, Being the Kahn Lectures for 1930*, Princeton, 1931; (c) *An Autobiography*, 1932, with references as reissued New York, 1943; and (d) Wright's articles in the Madison, Wis., *Capital Times*, February 1934 to October 1937; references are to excerpts reprinted in *An American Architecture*, New York, 1955. References for (a) and (b) are taken from *The Future of Architecture*, New York, 1954, where they are reprinted.

2 Louis Sullivan.

3 *An American Architecture*, 208.

4 Reprinted in Edgar Kaufmann and Ben Raeburn, eds., *Frank Lloyd Wright: Writings and Buildings*, New York, 1960.

5 *Future of Architecture*, 140.

6 *An Autobiography*, 143.

7 *Future of Architecture*, 140.

8 The earlier treatment in Arthur Drexler, *The Drawings of Frank Lloyd Wright*, New York, 1962, pl. 34; the final version in Henry-Russell Hitchcock, *In the Nature of Materials*, new ed., New York, 1973, fig. 120.

9 *An Autobiography*, 146.

10 *An American Architecture*, 209. The sentence sequence has been changed for emphasis.

11 This phrase was chosen as the title of H.-R. Hitchcock's indispensable book.

12 Wright became interested in refracted light in the 1890s when he held a franchise for Luxfer Prism glass blocks.

13 *An Autobiography*, 1943, 338–340. The sentence order has been changed.

14 *An Autobiography*, 341.

15 For a sampling of Garbett's ideas, see Edward R. De Zurko, *Origins of Functionalist Theory*, New York, 1957.

16 *An Autobiography*, 344, 345, 347.

Frank Lloyd Wright and Gottfried Semper

In the commentary on "Frank Lloyd Wright's 'Lieber Meister'" there is mention of the influence of Gottfried Semper on the architectural community in Chicago when Wright first worked there as a young draftsman. It seems doubtful that Wright knew about Semper directly, but Semperian ideas were among the concepts available to inquiring minds at that time. My own acquaintance with Semper's *Der Stil* allowed me to respond almost subconsciously to some of Wright's ideas when I joined his Taliesin Fellowship in 1934. This was not long after my exposure to Semper, guided by a remarkable painter and craftsman in Florence, Victor Hammer. His training, remote from Wright's concepts in many ways, was one I experienced in search of an education other than a regular college curriculum. This became a recommendation when I applied to Wright, to whom a lack of academic training was an indication of authenticity. Thus it may be of interest to add here some reminiscences (used by permission from Carolyn R. Hammer, [ed.], *Victor Hammer, An Artist's Testament*, Lexington, Kentucky, 1988):

Now as I conjure up those days of the early 1930s,...

my teacher, Victor Hammer, appears serenely busy, passionately clear, dispassionately wise....For him every phase of work, each material used, was a precious element in the consonance of form, supernal, redeeming, fruitful form. The essence of form, Victor averred, could be learned by relentlessly observing the visible world and works of art (selected ones to be sure) and by pondering the texts of two then forgotten theorists. One was Konrad Fiedler and the other, Gottfried Semper. I was aware of Fiedler's close associate, Adolf Hildebrand; his manual, *The Problem of Form,* was available in English and used in some art schools in the United States. But this did not prepare me for the delicate and profound philosophical essays of Fiedler, or Semper's densely factual, quasi-archaeological lucubrations.

To this I now add an esssay (printed by permission of the editors of a forthcoming *festschrift* honoring Vincent Scully, Jr.) on a neglected but central element of Semper's mature thought. In it Semper's underlying principles of design are directly linked to human physiology and hence to human instincts, feeling, and ideas. This appears attuned to Wright's concept of organic architecture, presented at the close of the section on "Plasticity, Continuity, and

Ornament." Semper's unfinished monumental treatise, *Der Stil*, was accepted as a master theory of architecture in German-speaking lands from the 1860s to the close of the century, when doctrinaire followers brought it into disrepute. In recent decades European scholars have again studied Semper's works exhaustively, yet one significant section has not received due attention, the axioms he added at the end of the Prolegomena to *Der Stil*.

In America Semper is appreciated mainly in two contexts: first, as a somewhat shadowy influence on Chicago architects active after the fire of 1871, and then, as the advocate of a paradigm adopted by the Prairie School there as the new century dawned—"the four elements of architecture," platform, hearth, enclosure, and roof. This idea had gradually matured into a concise unit of Semper's thought. However, in *Der Stil* he sought more fundamental values and chose his axioms; they raised questions about the meaning of architecture as a human activity, questions still alive today.

Semper's thought was indelibly marked by his experiences as a young man in the early 1830s in Paris, working among the German architects who had taken root there. His free time, he tells us, was spent roaming and pondering in the Jardin des Plantes, and especially in its museum of natural history arranged by the great Baron Cuvier to demonstrate his theories (mostly no longer accepted). Cuvier's display led Semper to believe that a patient analysis of nature would foster a command of form, and, moreover, that a clear, systematic theory was proof of truth. Then, in the mid '30s, Semper explored Greek architectural remains; he was enthusiastic about the new and controversial discovery of

their polychromatic enrichments.

More than twenty years later, as a prominent professor, he wrote in *Der Stil*, "the author assumes that basic concepts of aesthetics are known, but since he adopts personal interpretations of some aspects of them, he owes readers an elucidation which, as a mere supplement to a preface, must be limited to discussing certain terms used." Semper continued, "Magically, art of every kind enthralls the human spirit. The enchantment of an artwork is called beauty, but beauty is not truly an ingredient of art but, rather, an effect produced when all the characteristics of an art, inherent and conditioned, act in unison. These characteristics necessarily arise from and conform to the laws of nature. Albeit art is involved solely with shapes and semblances, not with the essence of things, nevertheless art can issue only out of what was learned from phenomena ruled by universally valid natural laws." Semper then named his "three factors of formal beauty, symmetry, proportion, and orientation." And these "correspond to the three dimensions of space— breadth, height, and depth. Just as it is impossible to conceive of a fourth spatial dimension [this was 1860] so it is not possible to define a fourth elemental factor of beauty."

Thus Semper posited his axioms, the three factors of formal beauty, and asserted their direct relationship to the structure of space itself. He had reason to believe that he was continuing on Cuvier's path. Two of the factors were blessed by ancient tradition and orientation, the third, needed to be explained. This would be achieved as he proceeded to demonstrate that the factors were analogous to spatial axes. For this task Semper decided to make use of a

third triad, the common division of natural phenomena into kingdoms: animal, vegetable, and
mineral. The last and lowliest of these was considered to include everything not specifically
animal or vegetable. There Semper found ex-
emplars to begin his thesis: a geode and a snowflake. These were fully centralized entities,
formed, he claimed, without external influence, and they would show that in primal natural structures the three factors of beauty were
present, singly or in combinations.

The geode and the snowflake presented obvi-
ous contrasts, but it was the qualities they held
in common that helped Semper to pursue paral-
lels in the laws of nature and those of art. The
geode was bulky, the snowflake was diapha-
nously flat: yet both were organized by rigor-
ously centric power. The crystals of the geode
pointed in, the rays of the snowflake thrust out,
yet both were defined by cores extending their
sway equally evenly throughout. The exem-
plars, complete in themselves, were not oriented toward any feature of the environment,
their orientation was fully self-referential.

Although subordinate to self-orientation,
symmetry and proportion were not lacking.
The geode could show symmetry at any cut
through its body; different crystals alternated
in regular sequences, and once a midpoint of
the section was selected, the same pattern
showed on either side of it. Symmetry appeared
to pass from right to left, or vice versa, and
Semper designated a horizontal line as the axis
of symmetry.

Here Semper introduced the vexed term,
eurhythmy, to which Vitruvius referred with
maximum ambiguity. Scolding the [as he be-
lieved] ignorant Roman, Semper presented the

true meaning, he said, of the Greek term. In
nature eurhythmy would be found in the sequence of crystals around the center of a geode,
and in Greek architecture in girdling ornamental motifs. These recur frequently, ranging
from simple bead moldings through egg-and-
darts, leafy garlands, even belts of triglyphs and
metopes, to elaborate gutters accented by rain-
spouts formed as lion masks, etc. The numerous
ornamental bands, "stimulating or soothing,
but never tiresome," helped unify the architectural whole.

Next, Semper considered the framing used
to articulate flat surfaces and to focus attention
on whatever appeared within them, i.e., door
and window cases or picture frames. Their
main duty was to clarify priority and subser-
vience. All were used as basic devices of design
at that time but after the modernist attack on
ornamentation, not often used and, then, less
skillfully. Semper sorted the components of
frames into two categories; first, framing
proper, eurhythmic, pointing in or out or both
alternately and, then, added features like pedi-
ments or consoles which, symmetrical or proportional, were addressed to the environment
and its inhabitants.

An odd aside may reflect Semper's long association with Richard Wagner; it claims that
music can be more sensitive and varied in its
organization than visual design since the ear is a
more delicate receiver than the eye.

Equally curious is a recapitulation where
Semper again declares that symmetry is but a
fragment of eurhythmy. In everyday experience bilateral balance appears to extend freely,
it does not enclose. Nevertheless the evidence
had to be fitted to the system: three factors of

beauty were to be acknowledged, the third had to be proportion. It shows in a single ray of the snowflake when the generative point is put below and the ray points upward. Branches emerge on each side and have lesser offshoots. The whole resembles a diagram of a tree. As in many trees the branching diminishes the higher it goes, indicating a contest of gravity with growth; their graded conciliation creates proportion. Semper designated the vertical as the axis of proportion.

Moving on into the vegetable kingdom, Semper looked at long-stemmed plants like trees. A bird's-eye view reveals a centric growth, perhaps modified by local conditions but always conserving the vital trunk. Seen at ordinary human eye level, the tree extends branches at apparently irregular intervals creating what is called occult balance since, however unobviously, the strains on the trunk must balance overall. A schematic diagram would also show how a leaf related to its twig as twig to branch, and branch to trunk. This establishes a secondary proportional scheme, complicated by the persistent, though dwindling, effect of the initial relationship, branch to trunk, on each subordinate one, and each of these on its sequels, diminuendo.

In the vegetable realm, orientation comes free of its confinement within a centric entity; now it relates to the environment. A tree grows toward light, along a radius aligned from earth's center of gravity to the sun. The same is true of any sessile organism, it reaches out into space. Proportion and orientation merge in one axis.

Looking back over Semper's examples so far two trends can be seen. First, he has begun to take notice of the exceptions and mutations of natural systems which inevitably occur in actuality; whether this might be reflected in the production of artwork remains unclear. Second, and Semper seems only fragmentarily aware of it, is the duality that marks his three factors. Orientation in the mineral kingdom can point inward or outward within the closed entity. In the vegetable kingdom orientation is vertical, growth is pointed up or down. It is remarkable that roots growing down are mentioned only in a casual aside, yet Semper did not ignore them entirely. Symmetry, in the first two kingdoms, remains eurhythmic, circular; bilateral balance is mentioned but not examined until animals become the topic. Proportion is always inherently dual, an adjustment of opposites. This pervasive dualism continues through his account of the animal kingdom.

In animals, mobility complicates the manifestations of the factors, but Semper proceeds, beginning with apods of the earth, the waters, and the air. He deals with their motions principally parallel to the surface of the globe, hence in the short run horizontality characterizes their orientation and in the same axis— proportionality expresses growth within a refraining ambiance. Apods also demonstrate the effect of gravity on the proportions of the animal: the belly hangs down below the horizontal spine, farther than the musculature rises above it. In apods, as in all animals, symmetry provides the requisite bilateral balance.

In quadrupeds dual proportionality is continued, bellies and chests hang down while thrusting foreparts are bulkier than rears. Orientation is essentially forward despite the need for agility.

The most advanced of all animals is mankind. Many structural features are derived from antecedent creatures but human axiality is unique, it lacks the doubling encountered hitherto. Human proportionality rises smoothly from the ground to the crown, while symmetry balances the form from side to side. These establish axes at a right angle one to the other, and at a right angle to both, orientation is focused forward. In humans each factor is clearly separate from the others, and only mankind is organized to respond to the spatial environment as a three-dimensional experience. Semper does not speculate on the implications of this, vast as they may be. He does, however, discriminate two types of human orientation—instinctive reactions and the operations of free will. A new dualism has been established.

This image of mankind, incorporating the three factors separately, might have served as the culmination of Semper's addendum, all the more as the demonstration of the factors at work in the designing of architecture and applied arts was meant to be a feature of the great opus being introduced. Semper opted to continue his argument by considering another of Vitruvius's ambiguous terms, authority. Each factor is granted its special authority; these prove to be very like the priority of one factor over the others, or of two combined over the remaining one. This had already received attention, as reported here. A fourth authority is now introduced superior to the three—the authority of character or purpose. This might be an echo of the doctrine of *architecture parlante,* or of the concept behind it, but the fourth authority is not investigated in any detail at this point.

Among several topics folded into the discussion of authorities, two may be mentioned. One is Semper's color theory influenced by his Grecian studies. Somber, earthy colors should be spread in broad masses below and, in a gradual, proportioned rise, the colors should lighten, clear, and brighten until an airy, vivid termination is achieved. The other is his sense of monumentality, closely modeled on the image of a center of power surrounded as occasion requires by rings of ancillary elements.

A limping end, readers may feel, to an arbitrary and inadequate theory. Nor would I disagree, yet with all the defects of Semper's ideas I believe they contain a seed of great insight. Semper grasped a fact, instinctively felt by naive enthusiasts of art, and often brushed aside by rational analysis, that the power of art, of its forms and of its programs, arises from subliminal sympathies and revelations. Semper sought to show how these were expressions of humans as naturally structured creatures. He aimed to explain how art itself is essentially a natural process rather than a preternatural contrivance. As Stephen Jay Gould of Harvard wrote, "good insights for bad reasons are legion in the world of intellect."

SOURCES

Semper, Gottfried, *Der Stil in den technischen und tektonischen Künsten, oder praktische Aesthetik,* vol. 1, Frankfurt a. M., 1860, vol. 2, München, 1863. Addendum to the Prolegomena, pp. XXI to XLIII. Second, revised edition, 2 vols., München, 1878, 1879. The addendum was unchanged.

Semper, Gottfried, *Die vier Elemente der Baukunst,* Braunschweig, 1851

Hermann, Wolfgang, *Gottfried Semper in Search of Architecture,* Cambridge, Massachusetts, and London, England, 1984. On pp. 219–44, "The Attributes of Formal Beauty," a translation of preliminary mss. notes for the addendum to the Prolegomena, under the heading, "Theorie des Formell-Schönen." These notes are not compared with the published text.

[Vogt, Adolf Max, et al., eds.], *Gottfried Semper und die Mitte des 19. Jahrhunderts,* Basel and Stuttgart, 1976.

Pevsner, Nikolaus, *Some Architectural Writers of the Nineteenth Century,* Oxford, 1972. Pevsner mentions Semper's interest in "symmetry, proportionality, and direction, co-ordinated with height, breadth, and depth," but says no more.

Gould, Stephen Jay, "Petrus Comper's Angle," *Natural History,* July 1987. The passage quoted occurs on p. 15.

I am grateful to the editors of a forthcoming *festschrift* for Vincent Scully, Jr., for allowing me to reuse my contribution, with minor changes, as the larger part of "Frank Lloyd Wright and Gottfried Semper." The original contribution was copyrighted in 1987 and sent to a few friends. In 1988 the Cambridge University Press issued *Gottfried Semper The Four Elements of Architecture and Other Writings,* translated by Harry Francis Mallgrave and Wolfgang Herrmann. This volume is introduced by Mr. Mallgrave in a brilliant survey of Semper's life and works, fully annotated. He shows that Semper's introduction to Cuvier's display and his subsequent trip to Italy and Greece should be dated one or two years earlier than I claim here. Furthermore, in the main text Semper's entire and prolix Prolegemena to *Der Stil* is lucidly translated but without any comment.

EDGAR J. KAUFMANN, JR.: PUBLICATIONS 1938–1989

Edgar J. Kaufmann, jr.: Publications 1938–1989

COMPILED BY ALFRED WILLIS

1938

1. (editor) "New directions in design." In *New directions in prose & poetry 1938*, ed. James Laughlin. Norfolk, CT: New Directions, 1938, [pp. 157–62 and twenty-two ills. on sixteen pls.].

A pictorial record of "scouting among new directions in daily living"; sets the tone of Kaufmann's numerous later critical writings on modern design.

1939

2. (editor) "New directions in design." In *New directions in prose & poetry 1939*, ed. James Laughlin IV. Norfolk, CT: New Directions, 1939, pp. 163–66.

Introduces essays by Sigfried Giedion, Monroe Wheeler, and Russel Wright, as well as a pictorial section comprising twelve illustrations on six plates.

1940

3. (editor) "The new design and public acceptance." In *New directions in prose & poetry, 1940*, ed. James Laughlin IV. Norfolk, CT: New Directions, 1940, pp. 259–65.

A wide-ranging essay on the general nature and purpose of design, especially in contemporary society, including remarks on Adolf Loos, Frank Lloyd Wright, and Gottfried Semper.

1941

4. "Modern design and public acceptance." *American Designers' Institute review* 1 (December 1941): 6–7, 20, 22.

5. [untitled contribution] *Retailing home furnishings*, November 10, 1941, sec. 2, p. 13.

1944

6. "On leave with Australia's art." *Art news* 43 (October 1–14, 1944): 11–12, 27.

Reviews recent paintings by G. Russell Drysdale, William Dobell, Elaine Haxton, Donald Friend, and others.

1945

7. "Coming home to the Carnegie." *Art news* 44 (October 15, 1945): 10–13.

Reviews the third Carnegie invitational exhibition of contemporary American art.

1946

8. "Bernard Smith. Place, taste and tradition: A study of Australian art since 1788." *Art bulletin* 28 (June 1946): 131–33.

Review of Bernard Smith, *Place, taste and tradition/A study of Australian art since 1788*, 1945.

9. (participant) "Conference on industrial design, a new profession, held by the Museum of Modern Art for the Society of Industrial Designers from November 11 to 14, 1946." Museum of Modern Art, New York, 1946.

Mimeographed.

10. "Francis Lymburner's drawings." In *Fifty drawings by Francis Lymburner*. Present day art in Australia (series). Sydney: Ure Smith Pty. Limited, 1946, [pp. 7–9].

Compares Lymburner's style of draftsmanship with that of Henri Matisse and other twentieth-century artists.

11. "Hand-made and machine-made art." *Everyday art quarterly* 1 (Summer 1946): 3–4.

Compares the esthetic qualities of hand-crafted and machine-made products.

12. "Hyman Bloom." *Art in America* 34 (July 1946): 120–27.

An appreciation of Bloom's paintings of the 1940s.

13. "Modern design does not need ornament." *College art journal* 6 (Winter 1946): 140–42.

Reply to an article by G. Hayden Huntley, "In defense of ornament," *College art journal* 6 (Autumn 1946): 29–36.

14. "Modern rooms of the last fifty years assembled for a circulating exhibition of the Museum of Modern Art." *Interiors* 106 (February 1946): 68–82.

15. "The Museum of Modern Art/Department of Industrial Design." *Bulletin of the Museum of Modern Art* 14 (Fall 1946): entire issue.

Describes the mission of the department, of which Kaufmann was the director; incorporates Kaufmann's "What is modern industrial design?" p. 3.

16. "Shipboard design." *Interiors* 106 (December 1946): 74–85.

Compares and criticizes the interior appointments of the S.S. *America* and the Cunard Line's *Queen Elizabeth*.

17. "The violent art of hanging pictures." *Magazine of art* 39 (March 1946): 108–10, 112–13.

A critical review of mid-twentieth-century installation design, notable especially for its coverage of Wright's design for Solomon R. Guggenheim's Museum of Non-Objective Art, publicized earlier in 1946.

1947

18. (with Philip C. Johnson) "American architecture: Four new buildings." *Horizon*, no. 93–94 (October 1947): 62–65.

Describes Frank Lloyd Wright's projects for the (Guggenheim) Museum of Non-Objective Art in New York, New York (1945), and a sports club for Huntington Hartford in Hollywood Hills, California (1946); Ludwig Mies van der Rohe's Administration and Library Building on the Illinois Institute of Technology campus in Chicago (1944); and Marcel Breuer's design for the Geller house on Long Island (1946).

19. "International competition for low-cost furniture design." *Bulletin of the Museum of Modern Art* 15 (Fall 1947): 13–16.
Unsigned announcement.

20. "Modern rooms of the last fifty years/assembled for a circulating exhibition of the Museum of Modern Art." *Interiors* 56 (February 1947): 68–82.
Also exists as an offprint.

21. "Moholy." *Arts and architecture* 64 (March 1947): 25.
A brief tribute to László Moholy-Nagy (1895–1946).

22. *100 useful objects of fine design 1947 available under $100.* New York: Museum of Modern Art, [1947].

23. "Summer furniture 1947." *Art news* 46 (May 1947): 32–35, 59–60.
Reviews some modern porch and garden furniture in current production.

24. "Undampened Wright." *Architectural forum* 87 (July 1947): 22.
Letter to the editor stating, contrary to a supposi-

tion published in an earlier issue of the magazine, that "Falling Water [*sic*] is not, and has never been, so damp as to be uncomfortable, despite its location near the water and deep down in a heavily wooded ravine."

1948

25. "Borax, or the chromium-plated calf." *Architectural review* 104 (August 1948): 88–93.
Traces the history of "streamlining" in vehicle and product design over the second quarter of the twentieth century.

26. "Finn Juhl of Copenhagen." *Interiors* 108 (November 1948): 96–99.
Reviews some of the designer's contemporary chairs and sofas.

27. "Industrial design standards: England's Council of Industrial Design." *Interiors* 107 (January 1948): 130–31.
Assesses the impact of the Council over the first two and one-half years of its existence.

28. "New lamps are lit in Europe." *Arts and architecture* 65 (October 1948): [26–28].
Reviews some new Finnish and Italian lamps.

29. "Russel Wright: American designer." *Magazine of art* 41 (April 1948): 144–45.
Reviews the furniture and interior design work done by Wright (1904–1976) in the 1930s and 1940s.

1949

30. "British Rayon Industry Center." *Retailing*

daily, 15 June 1949, p. 16.

Describes Maxwell Fry and Jane Drew's design of this facility in Upper Grosvenor Street, London.

31. "The exhibition rooms." In *An exhibition for modern living,* ed. A. H. Girard and W. D. Laurie, Jr. Detroit: Detroit Institute of Arts, 1949, pp. 72–85.

Describes model rooms by Alvar Aalto, Jens Risom, Bruno Mathsson, Florence Knoll, Charles Eames, and George Nelson, as well as garden furniture by various designers. See also Items 39, 46.

32. "Finland designs glass for 1949." *Art news* 47 (January 1949): 36–37.

Exists also as an offprint produced for Finland Ceramics and Glass Company, New York, 1949.

33. "Glass across the map." *Art news* 48 (June–July–August 1949): 46–47, 63.

Reviews new designs in glass from Steuben, Orrefors, Alvar Aalto, and J. and L. Lobmeyer.

34. "Good form for '50." *Art news* 48 (December 1949): 38–39.

Chronicles the *Exhibition for modern living* mounted by the Detroit Institute of Arts to showcase contemporary housewares and office equipment, as reinstalled, with additions, at the Museum of Modern Art.

35. "Have a seat." *Art news* 48 (September 1949): 29–36.

A pictorial history of the chair, from the thirteenth to the mid-twentieth century.

36. "Importing textures from the far corners." *Art news* 48 (March 1949): 34–37.

Describes textiles from Asia, Central America, the Caribbean, and Scandinavia.

37. "Industrial design in American museums." *Magazine of art* 42 (May 1949): 179–83.

Virtually a reprint of "Museums and industrial design." *Journal of the Royal Society of Arts* 97 (12 August 1949): 714–24, but with more and different illustrations. Cf. Item 42.

38. *Mimosa by Henri Matisse.* [New York]: Alexander Smith and Sons Carpet Co., [1949?].

A trade brochure describing a deep-pile wool rug exhibited at the Museum of Modern Art in 1949.

39. "Modern design in America now." In *An exhibition for modern living.* ed. A. H. Girard and W. D. Laurie, Jr. Detroit: Detroit Institute of Arts, 1949, p. 27.

Comments on the purpose and possible impact of exhibitions of objects of everyday use. See also Items 31, 46.

40. (with George Malcolm Beal and V. C. Morris) *V. C. Morris.* San Francisco: Morris Gift Shop, [1949?].

Includes the same text as appears in *Art News* 48 (February 1950): 42–44. Cf. Item 57.

41. (with René d'Harnoncourt) "Museums and industrial arts." *Museum* 2 (1949, no. 3): 150–54.

Includes parallel French and English texts.

42. "Museums and industrial design." *Journal of the Royal Society of Arts* 97 (12 August 1949): 714–24 and discussion 724–28.

A much expanded, revised, and illustrated version of "Museums and industrial design," *Museums journal* 49 (May 1949): 35–36. Added material includes, notably, observations on the place industrial objects historically have held in American museums and exhibitions. Cf. Items 37, 43, 44.

43. "Museums and industrial design." In *Museums in modern life: Seven papers read before the Royal Society of Arts in March, April and May 1949*. London: The Royal Society of Arts, 1949, pp. 26–40.
Reprinted from *Journal of the Royal Society of Arts* 97 (12 August 1949): 714–24 and discussion 724–28. Cf. Item 42.

44. "Museums and industrial design." *Museums journal* 49 (May 1949): 35–36.
Examines the problematic status of mass-produced artifacts in museums traditionally devoted to the conservation and display of fine art, as well as the changing relation of museums to the industrial-design community. Cf. Item 42.

45. "Of design and the man." *Art news* 48 (October 1949): 20–21, 54.
Announces the *Exhibition for modern living* at the Detroit Institute of Arts; illustrated with installation views.

46. "Selected objects in the exhibition." In *An exhibition of modern living*, ed. A. H. Girard and W. D. Laurie, Jr. Detroit: Detroit Institute of Arts, 1949, pp. 40–71.
Introduces and catalogs "a selection of well-designed objects that represent the positive values in civilization today." See also Items 31, 39.

47. "Western earth to graceful pottery." *Art news* 48 (May 1949): 40–41.
Describes ceramics by Carlton Ball of California.

48. "What is happening to modern architecture." *Arts and architecture* 66 (September 1949): 26–29.
An attempt to define modern architecture not in terms of the esthetics of the International Style but rather in terms of an approach that integrates "the expression of function, structure and beauty in a building." Kaufmann had been on the panel of a symposium on the question, "What is happening to modern architecture?" held at the Museum of Modern Art on February 11, 1948; see *Bulletin of the Museum of Modern Art* 15 (Spring 1948): 2–21.

1950

49. "Chairs, Eames, and chests." *Art news* 49 (May 1950): 36–40.

50. "Furniture." *Architectural review* 108 (August 1950): 127–29.

51. "Light, space, air: Photographs and plans." *New York Times magazine*, February 5, 1950, pp. 20–21.

52. "Museums point the way home." *New York Times*, September 24, 1950, pp. 6–7.

53. "The new-old crystal of Baccarat." *Art news* 49 (March 1950): 42–43, 65–66.
Outlines the history of glassmaking at Baccarat and characterizes the locality's contemporary production.

54. *Prestini's art in wood*. Lake Forest, IL: Pocohontas Press, 1950.
Describes the treenware of James Prestini.

55. *Prize designs for modern furniture from the international competition for low-cost furniture design.* New York: Museum of Modern Art, 1950.

56. *What is modern design?* Introductory series to the modern arts, no. 3. New York: Museum of Modern Art, 1950.

   Tokyo edition, n.d.; 2nd edition, 1954. Cf. Item 183.

57. "Wright setting for decorative art." *Art news* 48 (February 1950): 42–44.

   Reviews Frank Lloyd Wright's Morris Gift Shop in San Francisco (1948). Cf. Item 40.

58. (translator) "Frank Lloyd Wright and the conquest of space," by Bruno Zevi. *Magazine of art* 43 (May 1950): 186–91.

   Abridged from Zevi, *Frank Lloyd Wright* (Milan: Il Balcone, 1947), pp. 7–29.

1950–1955

59. *Good design: An exhibition of home furnishings selected by the Museum of Modern Art, New York, for the Merchandise Mart, Chicago.* 11(?) numbers. New York: Museum of Modern Art, 1950–1955.

   Records of the important series of exhibitions organized by Kaufmann to call attention to modern furniture designs in current (mass) production.

1951

60. "Contemporary Italian design: A *commedia dell'arte.*" *Magazine of art* 44 (January 1951): 16–21.

   Reviews an exhibition of contemporary Italian

arts and crafts (including furniture), discerning the whimsical qualities of many of the items shown; also exists as an offprint.

61. "Einführung." In *Industrie und Handwerk schaffen neues Hausgerät in U.S.A.* Stuttgart: Landesgewerbemuseum, 1951, [pp. 112–16].

   Catalog of an exhibition organized by the Museum of Modern Art and sponsored by the United States Department of State and the Economic Cooperation Administration.

62. "Frances Lichten. *Decorative arts of Victoria's era (1950).*" *Magazine of art* 44 (October 1951): 250.

   Review of Frances Lichten, *Decorative arts of Victoria's era*, 1950.

63. "Frank Lloyd Wright at the Strozzi." *Magazine of art* 44 (May 1951): 190–92.

   Reviews a photographic exhibition of Wright's work assembled by Oskar Stonorov, mounted in the Palazzo Strozzi, Florence.

64. (with Finn Juhl) "Good design '51 as seen by its director and its designer." *Interiors* 110 (March 1951): 100–103.

65. [preface to] "Design, designer and industry." *Magazine of art* 44 (December 1951): 320–25.

   The article consists of the transcription of talks given by Charles Eames and Herbert Bayer at the June 1951 Aspen conference on design.

66. "Wonderworks of Tapio Wirkkala." *Interiors* 111 (November 1951): 94–99.

   Describes some of the Finnish designer's experiments in plywood, as well as some of his creations in glass.

1952

67. *Design for use, U.S.A.: Objets usuels sélectionnés par le musée d'art moderne de New York.* XXIe Salon des arts ménagers, 28 février 1952–23 mars 1952. Paris: Service des relations culturelles de l'Ambassade des Etats-Unis, 1952.

68. "Great Danes in silver." *Art news* 51 (May 1952): 39–41, 61–63.
An appreciation of silverwork by Georg Jensen, Johan Rohde, Harald Nielsen, and others.

69. "Sybil Moholy-Nagy, *Moholy-Nagy; Experiment in totality*." *Magazine of art* 45 (January 1952): 44–45.
Review of Sybil Moholy-Nagy, *Moholy-Nagy; Experiment in totality*, 1950.

70. *Taliesin drawings: Recent architecture of Frank Lloyd Wright selected from his drawings.* Problems of contemporary art, no. 6. New York: Wittenborn, Schultz, 1952.

71. "Three new buildings on the Pacific coast." *Architects' year book* 4 (1952): 55–63.
Reviews the Charles and Ray Eames house (Santa Monica, California), the Visitors' Information Center (Portland, Oregon), and the V. C. Morris Gift Shop (San Francisco, California).

72. (compiler) "The word on design." *Interiors* 112 (December 1952): 116, 150, 152, 154, 156, 158, 160, 162, 164, 166.
Statements by Frank Lloyd Wright, Mies van der Rohe, Le Corbusier, and Walter Gropius.

1953

73. *Amerikkalainen koti 1953, Koti je taideteollisuus koonnut Museum of Modern Art, New York.* Helsinki: Suomalais-Amerikkalaisen Yhdistyksen, 1953.
The record of an exhibition of home furnishings in the collection of the Museum of Modern Art, incorporating an essay by Kaufmann, pp. 37–40; title given also in Swedish: *Det amerikanska hemmet 1953.*

74. *"Design in use."* New York: Georg Jensen, Inc., [1953?]. Reprinted from "Kay Bojesen: Tableware to toys," *Interiors* 112 (February 1953): 64–67. Cf. Item 76.

75. "Foreword." In "Good design 1953." *Interiors* 112 (February 1953): 84–95; (March 1953): 148–53; see p. 84.

76. "Kay Bojesen: Tableware to toys." *Interiors* 112 (February 1953): 64–67.
Characterizes Bojesen's personality and career, and highlights his recent productions in silver and wood. Cf. Item 74.

77. "Mackintosh and the modern movement." *Interiors* 113 (December 1953): 18–19.
Review of Thomas Howarth, *Charles Rennie Mackintosh and the modern movement*, 1953.

78. (translator) "Man, matter and space: On the architecture of Frank Lloyd Wright," by Joseph [i.e., Giuseppe] Samonà. *Architects' yearbook* 5 (1953): 110–22. Cf. Item 128.

79. *What is modern interior design?* Introductory series to the modern arts, no. 4. New York: Museum

of Modern Art, 1953.
    Japanese translation, 1955. Cf. Item 183.

1954

80. *American industrial design. Mostra del Museo d'Arte Moderna, New York.* Milan: United States Information Service, 1954.

81. (translator) *Conrad Fiedler's essay on architecture, with notes by Victor Hammer.* Translation notes by Carolyn Reading. Lexington, KY: Stamperia del Santuccio [i.e., Transylvania University], 1954.

82. "Fashion and the constant elements of form:." *Arts and architecture* 71 (July 1954): 27.
    English version of a talk given at Biel, Switzerland, in early 1953 and published in German as "Die Modischen und die konstanten Elemente der Form," 1954. Cf. Items 87, 136.

83. (with others) "Five years of 'Good Design'?" *Industrial design* 1 (August 1954): 22–30.
    A round-table discussion.

84. "The handweaver's place in the U.S. textile market." *Handweaver & craftsman* 5 (Fall 1954): 11–14, 44–45.

85. "Jensen and silver." In *Fifty years of Danish silver in the Georg Jensen tradition.* New York: Georg Jensen, Inc., [1954], pp. 2–9.
    Simultaneously published in Copenhagen by Schonberg.

86. "Moderne amerikansk brugskunst." In *Amerikansk brugskunst.* Copenhagen: Kunstindustrimuseet, 1954, pp. 5–8.

87. "Die Modischen und die konstanten Elemente der Form." In *Das Konstante und das Modisch; Vorträge gehalten an der Lagung des Schweizerischen Werkbundes in Biel, Herbst 1953.* [Biel?]: Schweizerischer Werkbund, 1954, pp. 39–43. Cf. Item 82.

88. "Scandinavian design in the U.S.A." *Interiors* 113 (May 1954): 108–13, 182–85.
    Reviews a traveling exhibition of contemporary Scandinavian furniture, ceramics, glassware, metalwork, woodenware, and Bakelite products.

89. (respondent to Vincent Scully, Jr.) "The Wright–International Style controversy." *Art news* 53 (September 1954): 48–49.

1955

90. (editor) *An American architecture,* by Frank Lloyd Wright. New York: Horizon Press, 1955.
    Selections from Wright's writings so arranged as "to make the principles and aims of Organic Architecture more generally available and understandable" ("Editor's note," p. 15). Quotations taken from this compendium were reprinted in the exhibition catalog, *Form givers at mid-century* (New York: Time, 1959), pp. 12–17, passim. Reprint, 1960.

91. "Bringing home the wealth of the Indies." *Art news* 28 (April 1955): 32–33, 62–63.
    Summarizes an exhibition at the Museum of Modern Art, of traditional Indian textiles, jewelry, ceramics, and other applied or decorative arts.

92. "Editor's note." In Frank Lloyd Wright, *An American architecture,* ed. Edgar J. Kaufmann, jr. New York: Horizon Press, 1955.

93. "Nakashima, American craftsman." *Art in America* 43 (December 1955): 30–33.

Reviews the New Hope, Pennsylvania, home and showroom of furniture designer George Nakashima.

94. "Tiffany, then and now." *Interiors* 114 (February 1955): 82–85.

A rediscovery of the work of Louis Comfort Tiffany (1848–1943), illustrated with examples of Tiffany's ceramics, glassware, and metalwork, mostly from Kaufmann's personal collection.

1956

95. *Craftsmanship in a changing world: An exhibition of U.S. industry and crafts.* Washington, DC: United States Information Service, 1956.

French version entitled *Artisans-techniciens aux Etats-Unis,* 1956.

96. "The fifth comfort." [jacket blurb for] *The Dunbar book of contemporary furniture.* [Berne, IN]: Dunbar Furniture Corporation of Indiana, 1956.

97. (editor) *Louis Sullivan and the architecture of free enterprise.* Chicago: Art Institute, 1956.

The record of an exhibition directed by Kaufmann, celebrating the centenary of Sullivan's birth.

98. "A restatement." In *Off the production line; an invitational exhibition of products designed by industry for you.* Akron, OH: Akron Art Institute, 1956, [p. 3].

99. (with Pietro Belluschi) "S.C. Johnson & son, Inc. Buildings, Racine, 1937–1939; 1944, Frank Lloyd Wright, Administration (eighth). Laboratory (tied for fourteenth)." In "One hundred years of signifi-cant building/2: Administration and research buildings." *Architectural record* 120 (July 1956): 203–6; see p. 205.

A brief assessment. See also Items 103, 104, 109, 112.

100. "Scraping the skies of Italy. A tower building, designed and now being built in Milan, puts a new look on the old American art of skyscraper construction." *Art news* 54 (February 1956): 38–41.

Announces the construction of Gio Ponti's Pirelli Building.

101. "Some recent U.S. design/for use in modern interiors." *Architects' yearbook* 7 (1956): 116–23.

Brief descriptions and illustrations of some contemporary American furniture and lamps.

102. [untitled contribution] In "The H. C. Price Tower." *Architectural record* 119 (February 1956): 153–60; see pp. 158–59.

On Frank Lloyd Wright's skyscraper in Bartlesville, Oklahoma; also exists as an offprint. Cf. Item 147.

103. (with John Knox Shear) "Ward W. Willitts house, Highland Park, Illinois, 1902, Frank Lloyd Wright (seventh)." In "One hundred years of significant building/5: Houses before 1907." *Architectural record* 120 (October 1956): 191–94; see p. 194.

A brief assessment. See also Items 99, 104, 109, 112.

1957

104. "Allegheny County Buildings, Pittsburgh, 1884–87, H. H. Richardson (tied for seventeenth)." In "One hundred years of significant building/8: Civic monuments." *Architectural record* 121 (January 1957): 169–72; see p. 172.

A brief assessment. See also Items 99, 103, 109, 112.

105. "Art nouveau—new again." *Architectural forum* 106 (May 1957): 122–26.

An assessment of Victor Horta's architectural work of the 1890s in Brussels.

106. "At home with Louis C. Tiffany." *Interiors* 117 (December 1957): 118–25, 183.

An assessment of Tiffany's work as an interior designer, illustrated with reproductions of vintage photographs.

107. "A century of modern design." *Arts and architecture* 74 (August 1957): 16–17, 31; (September 1957): 24–25.

An outline of twentieth-century trends, with an emphasis on their theoretical underpinnings.

108. "224 avenue Louise." *Interiors* 116 (February 1957): 88–93.

Describes Victor Horta's Solvay mansion in Brussels (1895–1900).

109. (with Alan Burnham) "F. C. Robie house, Chicago, 1909, Frank Lloyd Wright (tied for first)." In "One hundred years of significant building/9: Houses since 1907." *Architectural record* 121 (February 1957): 199–206; see p. 200.

A brief assessment. See also Items 99, 103, 104, 112.

110. "Frank Lloyd Wright 3 new churches." *Art in America* 45 (Fall 1957): 22–25.

Describes the designs for the Beth Sholom synagogue in Elkins Park, Pennsylvania; the Annunciation Greek Orthodox church in Wauwatosa, Wisconsin; and a Christian Science church in Bolinas, California.

111. "Kepes' new volume relates art and science; views present artistic dilemmas and hopes." *Architectural record* 121 (March 1957): 62, 67.

Review of Gyorgy Kepes, *The new landscape*, 1956.

112. "One hundred years of significant building/12: In summary." *Architectural record* 121 (May 1957): 203–8.

A critical analysis of the structures presented in the first eleven articles in a series published in *Architectural record* (June 1956–April 1957) and concluded with this one. See also Items 99, 103, 104, 109.

113. "The tradition of ornament in modern architecture." *House beautiful,* January 1957, 76–77, 93–94.

Sees in the work of early modern architects such as Frank Lloyd Wright, Louis Sullivan, Charles Rennie Mackintosh, and Victor Horta both precedent and justification for a revived use of ornament in contemporary architecture.

114. "Victor Horta." *Architects' yearbook* 8 (1957): 124–36.

An assessment of Horta's work in Brussels of the 1890s, incorporating a list of all of Horta's major works compiled by Jean Delhaye.

115. [untitled contribution] In *Brainpower quest,* ed. Andrew A. Freeman. New York: Macmillan (Cooper Union for the Advancement of Science and Art), 1957, pp. 28–29.

Speculates that "it may be that the people who are really imaginative and creative are those able to bridge the world of science and the world of art or even other worlds."

1957–1958

116. "The Inland Steel Building and its art." *Art in America* 45 (Winter 1957–1958): 23–27.

Describes the building in Chicago by Skidmore, Owings and Merrill, and highlights the Inland Steel Corporation's collection of modern art intended to be installed in its offices; exists also as an offprint, 1957.

1958

117. "Art nouveau and all that. . . ." *Industrial design* 5 (April 1958): 38–41.

A bibliographic essay reviewing recent literature on Art nouveau architecture and design.

118. "Art nouveau, yesterday and today." *New York Times magazine,* September 21, 1958, part 2, pp. 56–57.

119. "The Brooklyn Bridge and the artist." *Art in America* 46 (Spring 1958): 56–59.

On the Brooklyn Bridge as a subject of modern paintings and graphics scheduled for inclusion in an exhibition at the Brooklyn Museum.

120. "Constructive vision." *Progressive architecture* 34 (March 1958): 246, 248.

Review of Frank Lloyd Wright, *A testament,* 1957.

121. "Edward Godwin and Christopher Dresser: The 'esthetic' designers, pioneers of the 1870s." Makers of tradition, part 30. *Interiors* 118 (October 1958): 162–65.

Summarizes the careers and characterizes the works of these two vanguard British designers of the later nineteenth century.

122. (with others) "Eight design authorities . . . evaluate '59 cars." *Product engineering* 29 (December 1, 1958): 26–29.

Pithy comments on 1959 Buick, Cadillac, DeSoto, Ford, Chevrolet, and Dodge automobiles.

123. "Industrial design." *Encyclopaedia Britannica* 14th ed., revised, 1958, vol. 12, pp. 284–85.

Also appears in subsequent printings through 1970.

124. "Manson's Wright, volume 1." *Interiors* 117 (March 1958): 20.

Review of Grant C. Manson, *Frank Lloyd Wright to 1910 / The first golden age,* 1958.

1958–1959

125. "The form of space for art — Wright's Guggenheim Museum." *Art in America* 46 (Winter 1958–1959): 74–77.

Previews the building, with emphasis on its interior spatial qualities.

1959

126. "Architectural coxcombry or the desire for ornament." *Perspecta,* no. 5 (1959): 4–15.

An essay on ornament in modern and earlier architecture, noting the renewed interest in the 1950s in the question of architectural ornamentation.

127. "Editorial note." In *Frank Lloyd Wright / Drawings for a living architecture,* ed. Edgar J. Kaufmann, jr. New York: published for the Bear Run Foundation, Inc., and the Edgar J. Kaufmann Charitable Foundation by Horizon Press, 1959, p. 8.

States that the purpose of this book reproducing numerous examples of Wright's architectural drawings "is to bring to a larger number of people the pleasure of seeing Frank Lloyd Wright's architecture at the stages of conception and first formulation."

128. (editor) *Frank Lloyd Wright/Drawings for a living architecture.* New York: published for the Bear Run Foundation, Inc., and the Edgar J. Kaufmann Charitable Foundation by Horizon Press, 1959.

Published in celebration of Wright's birthday, this book incorporates Giuseppe Samonà's "The architecture of Frank Lloyd Wright" (pp. 10–19). The latter is an abridged variant of the translation published as "Man, matter and space: On the architecture of Frank Lloyd Wright." *Architects' yearbook* 5 (1953): 110–22. Cf. Item 78.

129. "Introduction." In *On designing,* by Anni Albers. New Haven: Pellango Press, 1959, [p. ix].
2nd edition, 1961.

130. "Machine technology." S.v. "Americas: Art since Columbus." *Encyclopedia of world art,* ed. Bernard S. Myers. New York: McGraw-Hill, 1959–1968, 1983, vol. 1 (1959), cols. 328–31.

Outlines the major trends in the history of industrial design in the United States.

131. [untitled guest editorial] *Furniture forum* 10 (Spring 1959): [iii–iv].
Includes a brief biographical sketch of Kaufmann.

132. [untitled contribution] In *Glass 1959: A special exhibition of international contemporary glass.* Corning, NY: Corning Museum of Glass, 1959, pp. 13–16.

1960

133. "The biggest office building yet . . . worse luck." *Harper's,* May 1960, pp. 64–70.

A very negative critique of the Pan Am Building in New York, with special attention paid to the impact of the building on its urban context, including a history of the controversial development of the design for this structure over the tracks of Grand Central Station.

134. "Centrality and symmetry in Wright's architecture." *Architects' yearbook* 9 (1960): 120–31.

135. "The design shift 1950–1960." *Industrial design* 7 (August 1960): 50–51.

A reexamination of the "twelve precepts of modern design" included in Kaufmann's *What is modern design?* (1950), in the light of developments in design theory and changes in taste during the 1950s.

136. "Fashion and the constant element of form." *Industrial design* 7 (March 1960): 59–60. Cf. Items 82, 87.

Abridged from *Arts and architecture* 71 (July 1954): 27. Cf. Item 82.

137. (editor, with Ben Raeburn) *Frank Lloyd Wright: Writings and buildings.* New York: Horizon Press, 1960.

Other editions 1968, 1974; Spanish translation, 1962; German translation, 1963.

138. "The guiding stars, 1940 and 1960." *Interiors* 120 (November 1960): 177–79.

Identifies and characterizes the most consequential trends in design in 1940 and in 1960.

139. "Nineteenth-century design." *Perspecta*, no. 6 (1960): 56–67.

Emphasizes aspects of nineteenth-century furniture design that seem to prefigure twentieth-century modern trends.

140. "Those who speak in steel and stone." *Saturday review*, May 14, 1960, 21–22.

Review of the Masters of World Architecture series, including: Frederick Gutheim, *Alvar Aalto*, 1960; Françoise Choay, *Le Corbusier*, 1960; George R. Collins, *Antonio Gaudí*, 1960; Arthur Drexler, *Ludwig Mies van der Rohe*, 1960; Ada Louise Huxtable, *Pier Luigi Nervi*, 1960; Vincent Scully, Jr., *Frank Lloyd Wright*, 1960.

141. "Wright, Frank Lloyd." *Encyclopaedia Britannica* 14th ed., revised, 1960, vol. 23, p. 808.

Also appeared in subsequent printings through 1973, and in modified form in printings of the 15th edition from 1974 through at least 1987.

1960–1961

142. "An American view of the arts of Denmark and Danish modern design." In *The arts of Denmark.* Copenhagen: The Danish Society of Arts and Crafts and Industrial Design, 1960–1961, pp. 99–106.

1961

143. "L'art nouveau and the natural accident." *Arts and architecture* 78 (September 1961): 26, 28.

Observations on the design qualities of natural and naturalistic patterns, as exemplified in some Art nouveau ceramic and glass vessels.

144. "Edward Wormley: 30 years of design." *Interior design* 32 (March 1961): 190.

145. "The fine arts and Frank Lloyd Wright." In *Four great makers of modern architecture / Gropius Le Corbusier Mies van der Rohe Wright.* New York: Columbia University, 1961, pp. 27–37.

The definitive edition, 1963; reprint of the 1963 edition, 1970.

146. "Modern industry keeps the homefires burning." *Interiors* 121 (August 1961): 8.

An amusing, tongue-in-cheek vision of the modern home of the year 2061.

147. [untitled contribution] In *Architecture in America: A battle of styles,* ed. William A. Coles and Henry Hope Reed. New York: Appleton-Century-Crofts, 1961, pp. 371–73.

Reprinted from *Architectural record* 99 (February 1956): 158–59. Cf. Item 102.

1962

148. "Arts and Crafts Movement." *Encyclopaedia Britannica* 14th ed., revised, 1962, vol 2, p. 484.

Also appears in subsequent printings through 1973.

149. "Design." *Encyclopaedia Britannica* 14th ed., revised, 1962, vol. 7, pp. 258–59.

Also appears in subsequent printings through 1970, and (unsigned) in printings of the 15th edition from 1974 through 1982.

150. "Design, 19th-century." *Encyclopaedia Britannica* 14th ed., revised, 1962, vol. 7, pp. 259–62.

Unsigned; also appears in subsequent printings through 1970.

151. "Design, 20th-century." *Encyclopaedia Britannica* 14th ed., revised, 1962, vol. 7, pp. 262–64.

Also appears in subsequent printings through 1970.

152. (with others) "Industrial design in American culture and its relationship to the arts." In *Industrial design and its relationship to the arts.* New York: American Society of Industrial Designers, 1962, pp. 20–33.

153. "Inside Eero Saarinen's TWA building." *Interiors* 121 (July 1962): 86–93.

Reviews Trans World Airlines' new terminal at Idlewild (now John F. Kennedy International) Airport, Queens, New York.

154. "Interior design: architecture or decoration?" *Progressive architecture* 43 (October 1962): 141–44.

A brief history of interior decoration and design from prehistoric times to the present, with emphasis on nineteenth- and twentieth-century developments; inserted into the transcription of a roundtable discussion on "The architecture of interiors" led by Thomas H. Creighton, pp. 140, 145.

155. (with Dorothy Wright Liebes) "Modern design in tapestry." *Encyclopaedia Britannica* 14th ed., revised, 1962, s.v. "Tapestry," pp. 802B–803.

Also appears in subsequent printings through 1973, though later with major revisions.

156. "Thonet, Michael." *Encyclopaedia Britannica* 14th ed., revised, 1962, vol. 22, p. 152.

Also appears in subsequent printings through 1973.

157. "Tiffany, Louis Comfort." *Encyclopaedia Britannica* 14th ed., revised, 1962, vol. 22, p. 209.

Also appears in subsequent printings through 1973.

158. "Twenty five years of the House on the Waterfall." *Architettura — cronache e storia* 8 (August 1962): 255–58, 259–62.

A classic description of Fallingwater in both English and Italian versions. Cf. Items 160, 210.

1963

159. "Ashbee, Charles Robert." *Encyclopaedia Britannica* 14th ed., revised, 1963, vol. 2, p. 569.

Also appears in subsequent printings through 1967.

160. (with Bruno Zevi) *La casa sulla cascata di Frank Lloyd Wright 25 ani dopo. Frank Lloyd Wright's Fallingwater 25 years after.* Milan: ET/AS Kompas, 1963.

Reprinted from *Architettura — cronache e storia* 8 (August 1962); 2nd edition, 1965; 3rd edition, 1966. Cf Items 158, 209.

161. "Chair and sofa." *Encyclopaedia Britannica* 14th ed., revised, 1963, vol, 5, pp. 236–39.

Also appears in subsequent printings through 1972.

162. "Cole, Sir Henry." *Encyclopaedia Britannica* 14th ed., revised, 1963, vol. 6, p. 44.

Also appears (though later in altered form) in subsequent printings through 1973, and in printings of the 15th edition from 1974 through 1987.

163. "Critique." In "Dulles International Airport." *Progressive architecture* 44 (August 1963): 87–101; see pp. 94–99.

A review of the Chantilly, Virginia, air terminal

serving the Washington, DC, area, designed by Eero Saarinen & Associates (1962).

164. "Designer for the corporate image." *Saturday review*, February 2, 1963, 38.
   Review of Eero Saarinen, *On his work*, ed. Aline B. Saarinen, 1962.

165. "Frank Lloyd Wright and the fine arts." *Perspecta*, no. 8 (1963): 37–42.

166. "Man-made America: chaos or control." *Industrial design* 10 (July 1963): 10.
   Review of Christopher Tunnard and Boris Pushkarev, *Man-made America: chaos or control*, 1963.

167. "Sincerity, simplicity mark presentation of famous Fallingwater to conservancy." *Water land and life* 5 (December 1963): 6–7.
   Announces the transfer of Fallingwater from Kaufmann to the Western Pennsylvania Conservancy. Cf. Item 223.

1964

168. "Gallé, Emile." *Encyclopaedia Britannica* 14th ed., revised, 1964, vol. 9, pp. 1098–99.
   Also appears in subsequent printings through 1973.

169. "Memmo's Lodoli." *Art bulletin* 46 (June 1964): 159–75.
   Examines the career of Carlo Lodoli (1690–1761) and Andrea Memmo's portrayal of his views on architecture in *Elementi di architettura lodoliana* (1834); also assesses the claim of Lodoli, advanced on his behalf by later commentators, to being a "'father' of functionalist theory." Errata: *Art bulletin* 46 (December 1964): 589. Addenda: *Art bulletin* 60 (December 1978): 743. The addenda are supplied in the form of a letter to the editor reporting research by Antonio Foscari.

170. *Tempo libero*. Tredecisima trienale di Milano. Milan: Esposizione triennale internazionale delle arti decorative e industriali e dell'architettura moderna, 1964.

171. [untitled contribution] *Design quarterly*, no. 61 (1964): 21.

1965

172. "Frank Lloyd Wright's years of modernism, 1925–1930." *Journal of the Society of Architectural Historians* 24 (March 1965): 31–33.

173. "How to look at architecture." *Harper's*, January 1965, 120–24.

174. "Some American architectural ornament of the Arts and Crafts era." *Journal of the Society of Architectural Historians* 24 (December 1965): 285–91.
   A study of the Fleur de Lys studios building, Providence, Rhode Island (1885).

175. "The Usonian Pope-Leighey house." *Historic preservation* 17 (May–June 1965): 96–97.
   An essay on the 1939 Usonian house moved from Falls Church to Woodlawn Plantation (Mount Vernon), Virginia (1964–1965). Cf. Item 185.

1966

176. "Crisis and creativity: Frank Lloyd Wright, 1904–1914," *Journal of the Society of Architectural Historians* 25 (December 1966): 292–96.

177. "Design sans peur et sans ressources." *Architectural forum* 125 (September 1966): 68–70.

An essay on the essential nature of design, especially as practiced in the nineteenth and twentieth centuries.

1967

178. "Canada's new turn in architecture." *Harper's,* May 1967, 62–68.

Reviews current trends in Canadian architecture, and provides critical descriptions of many pavilions at Expo 67 in Montreal.

179. "Twentieth-century architecture, the middle years 1940–1965, by John Jacobus." *Architectural forum* 127 (July 1967): 76–77.

Review of John Jacobus, *Twentieth-century architecture: the middle years 1940–1965,* 1966.

1968

180. "Introduction." In *Frank Lloyd Wright. The early work.* New York: Horizon Press, 1968, pp. xiii–xvi.

Reprint, [1971?].

181. [untitled contribution] In *Toledo Glass National II.* Toledo, OH: Toledo Museum of Art, 1968, p. 8.

1969

182. "Frank Lloyd Wright: The eleventh decade." *Architectural forum* 130 (June 1969): 38–41.

Reflections on recurring themes in Wright's ar-

chitectural work, including an appreciation of the subtleties of his late designs. Cf. Item 201.

183. *Introductions to modern design: What is modern design? What is modern interior design?* New York: Arno Press, 1969.

Reprinted from *What is modern design?* 1950; *What is modern interior design?* 1953. Cf. Items 56, 79.

184. "2001 B.C. to 2001 Centre Avenue." *Architectural forum* 131 (October 1969): 54–57.

The text of the Hans Vetter Memorial lecture at Carnegie-Mellon University, on the theme of the essential natures of architecture and architectural history.

185. "The Usonian Pope-Leighey house." In *The Pope-Leighy* [sic] *house.* Washington, DC: The National Trust for Historic Preservation, 1969, pp. 119–20.

Reprinted from *Historic preservation* 17 (May–June 1965): 96–97. Cf. Item 175.

1970

186. "Environment is an art." *Bulletin of the Metropolitan Museum of Art* 28 (April 1970): 321–30.

Summarizes Kaufmann's *Rise of an American architecture* exhibition. See Item 192.

187. "Introduction." In *The rise of an American architecture,* ed. Edgar J. Kaufmann, jr. New York: Praeger, and London: Pall Mall Press, 1970, pp. ix–x.

A plea for the preservation of America's historic buildings.

188. "Martin Battersby, *The decorative twenties,* . . . Giulia Veronesi, *Style and design, 1909–1929,* . . . Giulia Veronesi, *Stile 1925. Ascesa e caduta delle 'Arts Déco',* . . . " *Art bulletin* 52 (September 1970): 340–41.

Review of Martin Battersby, *The decorative twenties,* 1969; Giulia Veronesi, *Style and design, 1909–1929,* 1968; Giulia Veronesi, *Stile 1925. Ascesa e caduta delle "Arts Déco,"* 1966.

189. "Otto Antonia Graf: *Die vergessene Wagnerschule.*" *Journal of the Society of Architectural Historians* 29 (March 1970): 71–74.

Review of Otto Antonia Graf, *Die vergessene wagnerschule,* 1969.

190. "The rise of an American architecture/a book and an exhibition." In *The rise of an American architecture,* ed. Edgar J. Kaufmann, jr. New York: Praeger, and London: Pall Mall Press, 1970, pp. 221–37.

Outlines and summarizes the points made in Kaufmann's exhibition, *The rise of an American architecture.*

191. "'The rise of an American architecture.'" *Progressive architecture* 51 (April 1970): 80–81.

Summarizes the points made in Kaufmann's exhibition, *The rise of an American architecture.* See Item 192.

192. (editor) *The rise of an American architecture.* New York: Praeger, and London: Pall Mall Press, 1970.

Published in conjunction with the exhibition of the same title directed by Kaufmann and held at the Metropolitan Museum of Art; consists substantially of essays by Henry-Russell Hitchcock, Albert Fein, Winston Weisman, and Vincent Scully; simultaneously published in London by Pall Mall Press.

1971

193. "Herwin Schaefer. *Nineteenth century modern, the functional tradition in Victorian design.*" *Journal of the Society of Architectural Historians* 30 (May 1971): 183.

Review of Herwin Schaefer, *Nineteenth century modern / The functional tradition in Victorian design,* 1970.

1972

194. "Franco Borsi and Paolo Portoghesi. *Victor Horta.*" *Art bulletin* 54 (June 1972): 227–28.

Review of Franco Borsi and Paolo Portoghesi, *Victor Horta,* 1969.

195. [letter to the editor] *Art bulletin* 54 (June 1972): 235.

Apprises the scholarly community of the "ongoing destruction" of works by Victor Horta in Brussels.

196. [letter to the editor] In "On rethinking Wright." *Architectural forum* 137 (September 1972): 16; see p. 16.

One of five letters in response to Jonathan Barnett, "Rethinking Wright," *Architectural forum* 136 (June 1972): 42–47.

197. [untitled contribution] In "Viewpoints." *Interior Design* 43 (September 1972): 142–43, 150–51, 154–55, 160–61, 166–67, 170–71, 174–75, 182, 184; see pp. 142–43.

A personal opinion of the major trends in design from the 1920s through the 1960s, together with some predictions of future trends.

1974

198. "H. P. Berlage, idea and style, the quest for modern architecture." *Art bulletin* 56 (March 1974): 145.

Review of Pieter Singelenberg, *H. P. Berlage, Idea and style/The quest for modern architecture,* 1972.

1975

199. "The arts and crafts: Reactionary or progressive?" *Record of the Art Museum Princeton University* 34 (1975, no. 2): 6–12.

A critique of the theoretical underpinnings of the Arts and Crafts Movement.

200. [definitions relating to Renaissance and Modern architecture] In *Dictionary of architecture and construction,* ed. Cyril M. Harris. New York: McGraw-Hill, 1975.

201. "A profitable art." In *The art of design management: Design management,* ed. Thomas F. Schutte. New York: Tiffany & Co., 1975, pp. 31–39.

Another edition: *The uneasy coalition: Design in corporate America* (Philadelphia: University of Pennsylvania Press, 1975).

202. "Wright: The eleventh decade." In Frank Lloyd Wright, *In the cause of architecture,* ed. Frederick Gutheim. New York: Architectural Record, 1975, pp. 30–33.

Reprinted from *Architectural forum* 130 (June 1969): 38–41; another edition, 1987. Cf. Item 182.

1976

203. "The designer and education." In *Excerpts from papers presented May 20, 1975; John E. Walley Commemoration Design Conference on Human Dimensions.* Chicago: University of Illinois at Chicago Circle, 1976.

1977

204. [definitions relating to Renaissance and Modern architecture] In *Historic architecture sourcebook,* ed. Cyril M. Harris. New York: McGraw-Hill, 1977.

Reprinted as *Illustrated dictionary of historic architecture,* 1983.

205. "Who shapes the world? A view from the Place Beaubourg." *Artforum* 16 (November 1977): 60–61.

Reviews exhibits in the Centre de Création Industrielle of the Centre Georges Pompidou, Paris.

1978

206. "Frank Lloyd Wright: Plasticity, continuity and ornament." *Journal of the Society of Architectural Historians* 37 (March 1978): 34–39.

207. "Introduction." In *Frank Lloyd Wright's Fallingwater; The house and its history,* by Donald Hoffmann. New York: Dover Publications, 1978, [p. vii].

Dated February 1977.

208. "John McAndrew." *The Society of Architectural Historians newsletter* 22 (August 1978): 4.

Obituary of the head of the Museum of Modern Art's Department of Architecture and Design in the 1930s.

1980

209. "Precedent and progress in the work of Frank Lloyd Wright." *Journal of the Society of Architectural Historians* 39 (May 1980): 145–49.

1981

210. "The House on the Waterfall (1936/1962)." In *Writings on Wright/Selected comment on Frank Lloyd Wright,* ed. H. Allen Brooks. Cambridge, MA: MIT Press, 1981, pp. 69–72.
Adapted from the English text in *La casa sulla cascata di Frank Lloyd Wright 25 ani dopo. Frank Lloyd Wright's Fallingwater 25 years after,* 1963, pp. 20–25. Cf. Items 158, 160.

211. "'*Form* became *feeling*'; A new view of Froebel and Wright." *Journal of the Society of Architectural Historians* 40 (May 1981): 130–37.

1982

212. "Collecini, Francesco." *Macmillan encyclopedia of architects,* ed. Adolf K. Placzek et al. New York: The Free Press, 1982, vol. 1, pp. 438–39.

213. "Frank Lloyd Wright at the Metropolitan Musuem of Art." *Bulletin of the Metropolitan Museum of Art* 40 (Fall 1982): entire issue.
Incorporates a "Note" by Philippe de Montebello (p. [2]); an "Introduction" by R. Craig Miller (p. [3]); articles on "Frank Lloyd Wright's architecture exhibited" by Kaufmann (pp. 4–6) and on "Frank Lloyd Wright and Japanese prints" by Julia Meech-Petarik (pp. 48–56); along with illustrated descriptions of Wright-designed artifacts and building fragments in the collection of the Metropolitan Museum of Art. Kaufmann's article in this issue—published on the occasion of the installation of the living room of Wright's Francis W. Little house in Wayzata, Minnesota, in the Museum's American Wing—appraises the circumstances and influence of the many exhibitions of Wright's work held during the architect's lifetime and after his death in 1959.

214. "Frank Lloyd Wright's mementos of childhood." *Journal of the Society of Architectural Historians* 41 (October 1982): 232–37.

215. "Horta, Victor." *Macmillan encyclopedia of architects,* ed. Adolf K. Placzek et al. New York: The Free Press, 1982, vol. 2, pp. 421–29.

216. "Lodoli, architetto." In *In search of modern architecture; A tribute to Henry-Russell Hitchcock,* ed. Helen Searing. New York: Architectural History Foundation, and Cambridge, MA: MIT Press, 1982, pp. 31–37.

217. Lodoli, Carlo." *Macmillan encyclopedia of architects,* ed. Adolf K. Placzek et al. New York: The Free Press, 1982, vol. 3, pp. 17–20.

218. "Santos de Carvalho, Eugénio dos." *Macmillan encyclopedia of architects,* ed. Adolf K. Placzek et al. New York: The Free Press, 1982, vol. 3, p. 663.

219. "Wright, Frank Lloyd." *Macmillan encyclopedia of architects,* ed. Adolf K. Placzek et al. New York: The Free Press, 1982, vol. 4, pp. 434–48.

1983

220. "Wright at the Met." *Skyline,* January 1983, p. 25.

1984

221. "Aalto on First Avenue: A brief history of the Finnish master's lyrical conference suite." *Interior design* 55 (September 1984): 270–73.

Reveals Kaufmann's role in obtaining for Alvar and Elissa Aalto the commission to design a suite of conference rooms for the Institute of International Education, New York.

1985

222. "A true artist; Finland's Tapio Wirkkala, 1915–1985." *Interior design* 56 (August 1985): 196–201.

At once an obituary and a tribute to a virtuoso designer and artist.

1986

223. *Fallingwater, a Frank Lloyd Wright country house.* New York: Abbeville Press, 1986.

Incorporates "The house and the natural landscape: a prelude to Fallingwater," by Mark Girouard (pp. 14–23). Cf. Items 223, 224.

224. "Fallingwater at 50; Frank Lloyd Wright's masterpiece is fresh as ever after half a century." *Interior design* 57 (July 1986): 210–17.

Excerpts from *Fallingwater, a Frank Lloyd Wright country house* (New York: Abbeville Press, 1986) and from a 1963 speech on the occasion of the transfer of Fallingwater to the Western Pennsylvania Conservancy. Cf. Items 167, 222.

225. "How right was Wright." *House and garden,* August 1986, 140–45, 168, 170.

Excerpt from *Fallingwater, a Frank Lloyd Wright country house* (New York: Abbeville Press, 1986). Cf. Item 222.

226. "The object as elusion." In *American architecture: Innovation and tradition,* ed. David G. De Long, Helen Searing, and Robert A. M. Stern. New York: Rizzoli, 1986, pp. 30–31.

1987

227. "Semper's Axioms." Privately printed, New York, NY: 1987.

1989

228. "The Johnson Wax Building at 50; a stronghold of light." *Industrial design* 60 (February 1989): 236–37.

229. *9 Commentaries on Frank Lloyd Wright.* New York: The Architectural History Foundation, and Cambridge, MA: MIT Press, 1989.

The present volume incorporates the essay "Semper's Axioms," with minor changes, here entitled, "Frank Lloyd Wright and Gottfried Semper."

Illustration Credits

1–15. The Frank Lloyd Wright Archives

16. John Szarkowski, *The Idea of Louis Sullivan* (University of Minnesota Press, Minneapolis, 1956)

17, 18. The Art Institute of Chicago

19, 20. Author's collection

21. George A. Lane, S.J.

22. Edwin Smith

23. Weidenfeld & Nicolson Ltd.

24. Eastlake, *Gothic Revival*

25. By kind permission of *Country Life*

26. From *The Shingle Style* by Vincent J. Scully, Jr. (New Haven and London: 1955)

27. Bryan Shaw

28. From *The Architecture of H.H. Richardson and His Times* (The MIT Press, Rev. Edition, 1966)

29. *Art Gems from the American Architect* (Houghton Mifflin, 1887)

30, 31. Kornwolf, James D.: M.H. *Baillie Scott and the Arts and Crafts Movement*, The Johns Hopkins University Press, Baltimore/London, 1972, pp. 99, 107, 171, 209

32. 1895 First floor plan, which appears on page 5 of *The Oak Park Home and Studio of Frank Lloyd Wright*, written by Ann Abernathy, designed by John Thorpe/Oak Park, IL: The Frank Lloyd Wright Home and Studio Foundation, c. 1988

33, 34. Kornwolf, James D.: M.H. *Baillie Scott and the Arts and Crafts Movement*, The Johns Hopkins University Press, Baltimore/London, 1972, pp. 99, 107, 171, 209

35, 36. The Frank Lloyd Wright Archives

37. Daniel I. Larkin

38. Buffalo and Erie County Historical Society

39–47. Photographed by David A. Loggie — New York

48. Author's collection

49. From *Frank Lloyd Wright, The Early Work*, Horizon Press, 1968

50. The Frank Lloyd Wright Archives

51. Buffalo and Erie County Historical Society

52. The Frank Lloyd Wright Archives

53. Courtesy: William Clarkson

54. Buffalo and Erie County Historical Society

55. From *In the Nature of Materials: The Buildings of Frank Lloyd Wright, 1887–1941*

56. Author's collection

57, 58. From *In the Nature of Materials: The Buildings of Frank Lloyd Wright, 1887–1941*

59. From *Frank Lloyd Wright, The Early Work*, Horizon Press, 1968

60. *Brickbuilder*, August, 1901

61. Gilman Lane